Choosing
HOPE

Choosing
HOPE

Barry L. Johnson

Abingdon Press

Nashville

Choosing Hope

Copyright © 1988 by Barry L. Johnson

All rights reserved.

This book is printed on acid-free paper.

Library of Congress Cataloging-in-Publication Data

Johnson, Barry Lee, 1943-
  Choosing hope.

  1. Hope. I. Title.
BV4638.J64 1988   248.4   87-17564
ISBN 0-687-06705-7 (alk. paper)

ISBN 0-687-06705-7 (alk. paper)

Excerpt from "Courage" from *Collected Verse* by Edgar A. Guest. Copyright © 1934 by Contemporary Books, Inc. Reprinted by permission of Contemporary Books, Inc.

Excerpt from *Creative Brooding* copyright © 1966 by Macmillan. Reprinted by permission of Robert Raines.

Excerpts from *A Gift of Hope: How We Survive Our Tragedies* by Robert L. Veninga. Copyright © 1985 by Robert L. Veninga. By permission of Little, Brown and Company.

Song lyrics on page 191 from the collection *On Eagle's Wings* copyright © 1979 by North American Liturgy Resources, Phoenix, Arizona 85029

Excerpt from *Splinters in My Pride* by Marilee Zdenek, copyright © 1979. Used by permission of Word Books, Publisher, Waco, Texas 76796

"Turn Your Eyes Upon Jesus" by Helen Lemel. Copyright © 1922. Singspiration Music/ASCAP. Renewed in 1950. All rights reserved; used by permission of the Benson Company Inc., Nashville, Tennessee

Scripture quotations marked KJV are from the King James, or Authorized, Version of the Bible.

Scripture quotations marked RSV are from the Revised Standard Version of the Bible, copyrighted 1946, 1952, © 1971, 1973 by the Division of Christian Education of the National Council of the Churches of Christ in the U.S.A., and are used by permission.

MANUFACTURED BY THE PARTHENON PRESS
NASHVILLE, TENNESSEE, UNITED STATES OF AMERICA

For
John and Sally Hoppe
and the clan they began:
long on character,
rich in faith,
children of hope

Contents

Choosing
HOPE

Introduction

TOMORROW IS A RIVER

Nearly every summer our family makes its way to the tiny burg of Wild Rose, Wisconsin. My wife's parents have a delightful cottage on a small lake just a few miles outside this pastoral little villa. Not far from Wild Rose, State Route 22 crosses a happy little stream dubbed the Tomorrow River. The name has always been special to me, not just because it captures my imagination, but also because it perfectly reflects the character of this rivulet. The water is sparkling clear and always on the move, cascading over rocks, tripping through hairpin turns, and occasionally quieting over deep crevices.

Tomorrow is like that, the playground of the Holy Spirit, the land of hope.

Unfortunately, not all persons are so positive about tomorrow. Having been bruised by the weight of life, some folk cannot bear to look into the future. When they do, they see mushroom clouds, unemployment lines, city rescue missions, dialysis machines, and endless days of staring out of nursing home windows. For these people the Tomorrow River is a stagnant cesspool filled with the garbage of yesterday. As the

11

days pass it becomes more polluted, ultimately developing into a health hazard and eyesore for all who must endure it. This book is for those people and all who choose to love them.

A MATTER OF CHOICE

Hope is an option. It is not something with which we are born or a gift others can supply. It is something that must be chosen. Whereas we may not have any choice about what happens to us, we always have a choice about how to respond. I guess that was never more obvious to me than when I walked into the hospital room of a middle-aged man only minutes after he had been informed he was filled with cancer. A small-town businessman, this guy had developed the leading grocery store in the area. He had nursed it from a mom-and-pop corner carry-out to a huge, state-of-the-art supermarket. He was accustomed to claiming the future, finding a way, overcoming obstacles, surviving crises, choosing hope. Now, he was eyeball to eyeball with death. He chose hope again. "Barry, I figure I can treat this thing as a problem or an opportunity. I choose opportunity." He lived for at least a year longer than anyone anticipated. It would be nice to say he overcame all the pain, despair, and indignity that come with battling cancer. He didn't. All those things happened. He couldn't keep his food down. He lost his hair. And he gritted his teeth through indescribable pain. But, through it all, he never stopped choosing hope. Even in the last hours, he would smile about the promise of eternity.

Hope has that kind of influence on us. It takes some of the sting out of the present by pulling us into the future. Somehow, the chemistry of anticipation jumps all over the problems of the moment, reducing their magnitude, filling us with new perspective.

HOPE AND THE HOLY SPIRIT

There is a flow to all this which I believe is closely tied to the working of the Holy Spirit. It's almost like entrusting yourself to a tour guide. There is a sense of surrender in the process, but the end result is a more complete, fulfilling, informative experience than we can achieve on our own. Choosing hope is a way of boarding the Master's Grey Line cruiser. Sort of a confession: "OK, so I don't know everything. I will trust your guidance."

The process is like working on a blank canvas as opposed to painting by the numbers. In the second instance, there are few surprises and stiff, predictable results. But in the first, the spirit takes wing and the development of something new in time and quality—hope—is the consequence.

LETTING GO

Several years ago I was privileged to serve on a search committee for a church organist. It was a great experience, undoubtedly enhanced by the opportunity to visit many churches and hear a variety of organs. At last, we narrowed the choice to two persons and asked them to come to our church to play our organ. We scattered ourselves all over the sanctuary and enjoyed the concert. When it was concluded, the vote of the committee was unanimous.

Being a musical illiterate, on the committee solely because I was senior minister, I questioned the group as to why the decision was so clear-cut. The music director spoke up. "One was an artist, the other was a mechanic. The mechanic played all the notes with precision and accuracy. The artist put his soul into that organ!"

Such is the line between a life centered in hope and a life trapped in the present. Children of hope make a lifestyle of putting their souls into everything they do. They know how to let go. On the other hand, those who deny hope are damned by the dimensions of their perspective. They touch all the bases, play all the notes, fill in all the blanks, and end up wondering why life is so boring.

This week I received a call from a newspaper columnist wanting to pick my brain about the craft of preaching. After some basic questions regarding study habits and personal routines, he said, "OK, here's the biggie. How do you come up with something meaningful week after week after week?"

As soon as he asked the question, my mind raced to the sessions I so often enjoyed with seminary students in Dayton, Ohio, who came to me for preaching seminars. Early on, each student would ask that same question.

I always answered the same way: "We are insufficient as preachers until we admit our insufficiency."

Often I will stand in the shower on Monday morning attempting to piece together the message for the coming Sunday. I find it impossible. Even if I know the text and have the title—which is usually the case—I still can't figure out where to go with it. Only after studying the language, reading the commentaries, dissecting key words, and offering the prayer of hope—"Lord, this is yours, do with it as you please"—do I feel competent to put anything on paper.

In other words, only when I release control does God take control; only when I consent to follow the Spirit do I find the Spirit.

And so it is with choosing hope. Tomorrow is a river, filled with unexpected developments, constantly on the move, never to be trapped, never to be mastered. In that knowledge, ours is the challenge to admit our incompetency and claim the guidance of the Holy Spirit. For believers, until we confess what we cannot achieve, we will never know what we can. Until we choose tomorrow, we cannot release tomorrow. And until we release tomorrow, we cannot fully experience today.

FEAR NO MORE

When the Nazis occupied France during World War II, most of the French artistic community was forced underground. Unwilling to stifle their creativity and to paint by Hitler's numbers, these writers, musicians, and painters were hunted down by the Gestapo. Tristan Bernard was among the less fortunate. Although he and his family managed to elude their pursuers for several months, they were finally captured. As they were marched into prison, the French novelist turned to his wife and said, "The time of fear is over, now comes the time of hope."

Choosing hope means not choosing fear. It means looking every predicament, even death, squarely in the eye and proclaiming, "I can do all things through Christ who strengthens me."

I recall the refreshing approach of a golfing friend, in his late seventies. Every day he would sit down at the luncheon table with the rest of us and whip out the obituary column of the local newspaper. Running his finger down the ages of the deceased, he would play an imaginary match. For every one younger than he was, he would assume a win: "I'm up one." For every one older than he was, he would take a loss: "I'm down one." It was a humorous scene, but one with a healthy message. A child of hope, he was free to jest about the inevitable and thereby able to thoroughly enjoy the day.

So choosing hope is a therapeutic process. Although it centers in the future, it has tremendous returns right now.

Hence, we arrive at a final concern which shaped my thought throughout my research and writing.

Back in 1961, Martin Marty wrote a small book entitled *The Improper Opinion,* in which he examined the preacher's paradox: the pursuit of popularity on one hand, and the demand to preach the truth on the other. Marty was particularly concerned about those pulpiteers who speak to large groups. He observed, "The greater the congregation, the more restricted the pulpit." At First Community Church I wrestle with this issue every week.

Like Nathan confronting David, Elijah against Baal, Martin Luther before the Pope, and Martin Niemöller eyeball to eyeball with Adolf Hitler, it is the preacher's challenge to boldly share the truth as he or she sees it. There is no room for compromise or the accommodation of power. We are called to assess the society in which we live, to acclaim the noteworthy and confront the degenerate, to afflict the comfortable and comfort the afflicted.

The legendary preacher P. T. Forsyth put it this way:

You hear it said, with a great air of religious common sense, that it is the man that the modern age demands in the pulpit and not his doctrine. It is the man that counts and not his creed. But this is one of those shallow and plausible

16

half-truths which have the success that always follows when the easy, obvious underpart is blandly offered for the arduous whole. To be ready to accept any kind of message from a magnetic man is to lose the Gospel in mere impressionism. It is to sacrifice the moral in the religious to the aesthetic. And it is fatal to the authority of the pulpit or the Gospel. The Church does not live by its preachers, but by its Word. (Lyman Beecher Lectures, Yale University, 1907)

That Word is not always pleasant to hear. It does not massage the status quo at the expense of integrity. Rather, it stands as a lighthouse amidst the treacherous coves of power and comfort, telling us where we are, confirming, at one and the same time, danger and position.

What is at stake here is the *focus of devotion* for the mass of Americans. The most popular preachers of our time are those who depict success as God's answer to human effort. They tell us to hang tough, invest wisely, reach for the moon, and go for the best. They massage our fixation on material security and send us forth buttressed for Wall Street, bankrupt for the Damascus Road. They write books about reaching goals, overcoming life's problems, and being the best in our chosen field of endeavor. But, somehow, they look the other way when Bathsheba enters the room. They never make us deal with God's position in our hierarchy of values.

A few years ago, I enjoyed three days of intensive study at a monastery, in pursuit of my doctor's degree. One of the seminars offered had to do with "theology and today." I sidled into the classroom, ready to hear a multisyllabic analysis of the existential predicament paralyzing the souls of modern believers. I got a surprise.

Through thick glasses, a relaxed professor studied

each of us in the room. At last, he spoke: "Most of you have come here to wrestle with words and toy with theory. Bridging the gap between the Creator and the Created is simply not that complicated. If you would hold theological truth against current lifestyles, you need ask only one question, 'What's in it for God?' "

I sat there mesmerized by the simplicity. Stirring in my mind was Karl Barth's answer, when he was asked upon his retirement to summarize his theology. He said, "Jesus loves me, this I know, for the Bible tells me so!"

What's in it for God?

Believe me, that question overshadowed every word I nestled into this manuscript. If we are to build bridges between the Creator and the Created, it is the paramount question.

I believe Senator Mark Hatfield gives us the best evaluation of our dilemma.

In a collective sense, we are threatening to become the emotional by-products of society's one-dimensional exaltation of scientific and technological achievement. Dazzled by material success, we have developed a new religion: the worship of progress itself. Whereas people once looked toward God for salvation, they now direct their daily lives toward the domination of nature and fellow human beings in a ceaseless quest for economic prosperity. The worship of the supernatural, the mystical and unknown element of life, has been transformed into a worship of the visible, the tangible, the synthetic. (*Between a Rock and a Hard Place* [Waco, Tx.: Word, 1976], p. 157)

Now, mind, you, I have nothing against progress and success. To be sure, I invest a great deal of time and energy in pursuit of both. But neither deserves to so command my allegiance as to render my relationship to Christ pedestrian.

This is the issue the Gallup organization isolated with the 1976 survey of religion in America. They determined that the United States is the most "religious" developed country on the face of the earth. This is based on the high percentage of Americans who believe in God and an afterlife, who attend church or synagogue regularly, and who declare that religious belief is an important aspect of their lives.

Still, when Gallup finished his survey he was compelled to ask: "Are we really as religious as we appear? Or are we perhaps only superficially religious?"

Religious analyst Richard Quebedeaux offers a response to that question.

We may be outwardly religious, but the secular world would seem to offer abundant evidence that religion is not greatly affecting our lives. The United States has one of the worst records in the world in terms of criminal victimization. We live in a "ripoff society" marked by consumer fraud, political corruption, tax cheating, bribery and payoffs, to name just a few of the contemporary problems in America that are inconsistent with religious values.

Furthermore, while Americans may be impressively religious with respect to belief and outward manifestations, Gallup's surveys indicate a wide gap between religious belief and practice in our nation. (*By What Authority?* [New York: Harper & Row, 1982], p. 146)

It is to the people who occupy that gap that *Choosing Hope* is directed. During the course of my ministry I have watched too many people who talk the faith fail to find it when they need it most. Perhaps, as those of us who occupy the pulpits of Christ's church go about our business, we have overlooked that key question, What's in it for God? Maybe we have been too concerned with being popular to worry about being correct. For whatever reason, I sense we have not succeeded in communicating the hope at the heart of the Good News.

I pray that this work will serve as a bridge between the unfailing power of God and the nauseating despair of those who know not the touch of Christ's hand.

An old man going a lone highway
Came at the evening, cold and gray,
To a chasm vast and wide and steep,
With waters rolling cold and deep.
The old man crossed in the twilight dim,
The sullen stream had no fears for him;
But he turned when safe on the other side,
And built a bridge to span the tide.

"Old man," said a fellow pilgrim near,
"You are wasting your strength with building here.
Your journey will end with the ending day,
You never again will pass this way.
You've crossed the chasm, deep and wide,
Why build you this bridge at eventide?"

The builder lifted his old gray head,
"Good friend, in the path I have come," he said,
"There followeth after me today
A youth whose feet must pass this way.
The chasm that was nought to me
To that fair-haired youth may a pitfall be;
He, too, must cross in the twilight dim—
Good friend, I am building this bridge for him."
        (William Allen Dromgoole, "The Bridge Builder")

That's the real challenge of choosing hope in our time: to be ever aware that others will follow . . . and to go even further. My concern is to initiate thought, fan the embers of creative risk, and enable my readers to overcome the shackles of despair through the timeless promise of a power that will not be vanquished, the power of a risen Lord.

In closing, I offer my heartfelt thanks to those who enabled the assembling of these thoughts. It comes to me that no minister of a large church would ever be able to write without the blessing of a competent staff. No problem here. Jeb Magruder, Kline Roberts, Bill Hensley, and Dick Flynn have all helped shoulder ministerial duties while I was poking and pecking on my word processor. My long-time secretary, Nancy Buhr, has kept the calendar appropriately cleared, not to mention investing several hours cleaning up the manuscript. Meanwhile, my family has accepted my absence both physically and mentally during the matriculation surrounding this text. And finally, I offer a special word of gratitude to my faith-filled friend Barbara Riley, who, with the touch of grace and beauty which seems so natural to her, dissected and digested this manuscript several times over in an effort to make it as readable and real as possible. To all these people I bow in humble appreciation.

Barry L. Johnson
Columbus, Ohio
1987

1

A Matter of Choice

THE BASIC INGREDIENT

Greek legend tells us that Zeus, the sternly righteous governor of the world, once provided his subjects with an urn filled with everything necessary to be whole and happy persons. So overjoyed were the recipients of these treasures that they began to dance exuberantly, subsequently dropping the urn. The lid popped off and all save one of the life-shaping ingredients escaped. The people sat bewildered before Zeus. "Well," asked the all-powerful God, "what is left?" Peeking inside, one of the people replied shyly, "Only hope," to which Zeus retorted, "It is enough."

In this day, when the gap between the people of the penthouse and the people of the pavement seems to expand daily, the issue of hope is of paramount concern for all of us. It crosses racial, religious, and socioeconomic lines. I am fortunate to live and serve among people for whom shelter, food, and comfort are readily available. Still, even with such needs met, I have noted the phenomenal importance of hope. I have seen it on cancer wards when the odds are ninety to one against a cure and brave people reach for the courage to fight for life. I have seen it in the eyes of a heartbroken mother whose son was last seen in a helicopter tumbling into the underbrush of South Vietnam. And I have seen it in the eyes of a father whose fifteen-year-old daughter simply failed to come home—fifteen years ago.

Currently, a fresh rash of hope-starved situations clutter the front pages of our newspapers. What of the besieged farmers in America's heartland? What of the silently condemned victims of AIDS? And what of the mounting number of homeless street dwellers, for whom only the grace of others and the leftovers of an affluent society provide sustenance?

SENSITIZED BY TRAUMA

For all of us, the significance of hope is most often paralleled by the difficulty of our current situation. We don't think much about the importance of confidence in the future until the present is overloaded with seemingly insurmountable problems. For the most part, we bop along in our predictable little rhythms, oblivious to the need for spiritual/philosophical foundations, until we smack into the wall of disaster. Then we reach for something extra, but having failed to tend the garden of hope, it is extremely difficult to take nourishment from it.

In his book *A Gift of Hope*, Robert Veninga relates the powerful story of one who smacked into such a wall and came up with an appropriate response.

Marie Fisher was brought to a hospice to die. Seven thousand rads of high energy radiation could not stop the cancer from spreading throughout her body. The hospice seemed to be the last stop for this frail fifty-three-year-old woman, depleted after months of therapy.

Upon being escorted to her room Marie made the observation that, while everyone expected her to die, it wasn't exactly what she had in mind. With a hint of fire in her eyes she informed the head nurse that she was going to get well. What's more, she intended to leave the hospice not in a wheelchair, but on her own strength.

Two days later Marie's health was rapidly failing. A nurse speculated that her heart was simply giving out. She developed a severe breathing disorder and there was general recognition that she wouldn't last out the night.

Marie, however, would not cooperate with death. Deep in her being was a tenacious hold on life that was more powerful than the forces that were pushing her to die.

An oncologist who was monitoring her condition shook his head in disbelief as he listened to a heartbeat that grew steadily stronger. A nurse noted that the vital signs were beginning to stabilize. When it was announced that Marie's blood pressure had reached 110/80, a quiet cheer went up in her room. "She simply wouldn't give up," said her physician.

In the weeks that followed Marie was determined to get out of bed and walk a few steps every day. She was equally determined to set new goals for herself, for, after all, there were people she wanted to see and a huge stack of paperback novels that needed to be read.

But then came the setback. The cancer had spread into her pancreas. Not even high doses of morphine could control the pain.

An oncologist indicated that a surgical procedure might alleviate some of the discomfort. "However," he cautioned, "you should know that you are not a good surgical risk. Just getting you through the anesthetic would be an accomplishment."

Alone with her thoughts, Marie examined her options. An hour later she signed the forms permitting the surgery to take place. She reasoned there was a pretty good chance that the surgery might bring relief. More important, it might give her added life. The next day she successfully completed a three-hour operation.

While there was no sign of remission, Marie's bodily functions gradually returned to normal. "I'm feeling stronger every week," she confided to a roommate. Soon she was walking with little pain. Then she abandoned her hospital gown in favor of street clothes, for, as she told a nurse, "A hospital gown is a symbol of sickness." And then she asked the question that had been on her mind ever since she had entered the hospice: "When can I go home?"

"I'll never forget the day Marie left the hospice," said Catherine Holmberg, the chief nurse in the unit. "Marie was radiant. She put on a bright red dress accented with a white scarf. You could tell that she was proud of every step she was taking. If there was any pain she wasn't going to tell anybody about it.

"The word quickly spread that Marie was leaving. The patients came out of their rooms and the nurses stopped all their tasks as they watched her walk down the hall with her head held high. Then someone started to clap. Pretty soon we all joined in. A few tears ran down the cheeks of some of the nurses. All we could do was marvel at her courage. She had survived. ([Boston: Little, Brown and Co., 1985] p. 11)

CHOOSING HOPE

What sets a woman such as this apart from those who collapse at the first sign of difficulty? I choose to believe that the difference between life and death for Marie Fisher was the difference of hope. Because she was willing to claim a future, she had one. You and I face the same choice every time we encounter adversity. We can throw up our hands in despair, accepting the inevitability of disaster, or we can lay claim to a higher level of power that will enable us to cope with our problems no matter their magnitude. This is choosing hope. It is the difference between living from one crisis to the next and living with the planned abandon of those who are unconditionally loved.

In *A Tear and a Smile*, Kahlil Gibran describes his feelings as he sat on a hillside between a teeming city and an ancient graveyard. Even as he watched, his brooding was interrupted by the funeral procession of an obviously wealthy person. It was complete with multiple priests, incense burners, musicians, and a knot of mourners. The service lasted a long time, overflowing with eulogies and poetry, music, and frequent demonstrations of grief. And then they were gone, leaving only a mound of carefully ordered flowers around a resplendent marble stone.

Then, a crystallizing moment—he writes:

> The sun inclined toward the west, and the shadow of rocks and trees lengthened and Nature began to shed her garments of light. On that very moment I looked and beheld two men bearing a wooden casket. Behind them came a woman in rags carrying a suckling child. By her side trotted a dog, looking now at her, now at the casket. It was the funeral procession of a poor man, a humble man. There went a wife shedding tears of grief and a child who wept at his mother's weeping, and a faithful dog in whose steps were a pain and a sadness.
>
> They came to the burial ground and laid the coffin in a grave dug in a corner far from those marble headstones. Then they returned in silence, while the dog looked back at the last resting place of his good companion. And so till they vanished from my sight beyond the trees.
>
> And I looked toward the city, saying within myself: "That belongs to the wealthy and the mighty." And toward the graveyard I said: "This too belongs to the wealthy and the mighty. Where then, O Lord, is the home of the poor and the weak?"
>
> Having thus spoken, I lifted my eyes to the clouds, whose edges were colored with gold by the rays of the setting sun. And a voice within me said: "Yonder." ([New York: Alfred A. Knopf, 1950] pp. 16-17)

Hence, the line between the "haves" and the "have-nots" is obliterated by the need for hope. That "yonder" gripping us by the soul is the spectrum of hope. It has nothing to do with race, creed, or financial resources. All humans need it.

Carl Rogers, the renowned therapist, explains that people are much like potatoes in a basement; so long as there is a glimmer of light, they will develop sprouts and reach for it. Hence comes an echo across two thousand years of history, "The light shines in the darkness, and the darkness has not overcome it."

THE ADVANTAGE OF FAITH

Here is where people of faith have a distinct advantage. You see, in Jesus Christ, we find a hope against hope; a hope that reaches beyond the margins of our knowledge; a hope that breaks the bonds of human existence and offers the keys of eternity.

What is it?

What are its hallmarks?

How do we claim it?

For starters, we need to understand that Christian hope has a nature all its own. Jacques Ellul, the French theologian, puts it this way:

It must be remembered, of course, that Christian hope is more than a vague hope that things will be better tomorrow, or a stupid obstinacy that it will work out successfully next time, or confidence in human nature that it will survive the next test too after getting through so many, or the assurance which is based on a philosophy of history. Christian hope is none of these things. It does not rest on man or on objective mechanisms. It is a response of man to God's work for him. (*The Ethics of Freedom* [Grand Rapids: Wm. B. Eerdmans, 1976], p. 12)

In other words, God acts, we react. God demonstrates a love that smashes the limitations of human existence, and we in response function on a wholly different plane, a plane characterized by positive expectation, trust, and patience.

POSITIVE EXPECTATIONS

I have a banker friend who shared an anecdote that has shaped his thinking for years. Back when America was still on the grow, with the West still being won, a government agent was standing in a general store when a homesteader approached the proprietor for a line of credit.

"Are you doing any fencing this spring, Josh?" asked the storekeeper.

"Sure am, Will," said the rancher.

"Fencing in or fencing out?"

"Fencing in. Taking in another 360 acres across the creek."

"Good to hear it, Josh. You have the credit. Just tell Henry out back what you need."

The agent couldn't make much sense of this. "I've seen all kinds of credit systems," he said, "but never one like that. How does it work?"

"Well," said the storekeeper, "it's like this. If a man's fencing out, that means he's running scared with what he's got. But if he's fencing in, he's growing, expecting good things. He's got hope. I always give credit to a man who's fencing in."

That is positive expectation, a mark of the hope-filled person.

People of hope make it a point to fence *in* rather than *out*. It's the classic issue of optimism versus pessimism, positive versus negative, hope versus despair.

When I was crisscrossing the country doing church

renewal work in the early seventies, I learned to spot the difference in both people and churches. If they were looking to the future, they rarely had difficulty with new challenges. But if they had decided to be content as they were, the slightest bump in the road wreaked havoc.

The first challenge of Christian hope is that of "fencing in" rather than "fencing out." It's a matter of confidently approaching new adventures, knowing all the while that God is in charge, and that no matter what, the Creator's love will prevail.

INEVITABLY OPEN

Robert McAfee Brown explains the spirit of Protestantism as "constant openness to renewal at the hand of the Holy Spirit." This is also the spirit of Christian hope. Because Christ is victor we are free to explore all options with nothing to lose. We live offensively rather than defensively. We need never circle the wagons, because we are confident no force can defeat us.

This is what the author of Hebrews was lifting up when he wrote, "We have this as a sure and steadfast anchor of the soul, a hope that enters into the inner shrine behind the curtain, where Jesus has gone as a forerunner on our behalf" (Hebrews 6:19ff.).

In order to understand this thought, we must note that the writer is comparing the restrictions of the Temple to the limitations of life. The most sacred of all places in the Temple was the Holy of Holies. It was separated from the commoners by a veil. Entrance was denied everyone save the High Priest, and he could enter the Holy of Holies only on the Day of Atonement. There he entered the full presence of God.

We, as finite human beings, are separated from the full presence of God by the veil of death. In Christ, that veil has been removed and we are promised full access to Almighty God. Because Christ has interceded on our behalf, we need never "fence out" life.

RELEASING CONTROL

In this light, the second aspect of our hope is a willingness to trust God and resist the incessant human need to control. Again, it is Ellul who tells us "the attitude of power, of control, of rigidity, is a negation of hope."

Think about that for a moment. Are we not most hopeless when we are most manipulative? Do we not forego unexpected bliss when we attempt to structure predictable circumstance? Are we not most miserable when our only hope is ourselves?

In this sense, I find it very easy to identify with Thomas. You recall he was the disciple so dominated by his own conditioned responses that he simply could not believe Christ had conquered the grave. Consequently, Thomas could not hope.

Well, we are all creatures of conditioned responses, often trapped by our own experiences.

When the phone rings, we answer it.

When the light turns red, we stop.

When the clock says it is noon, we eat.

It does not matter if the caller is a lightbulb salesman from Syracuse, or if it is three o'clock in the morning at the red-lighted intersection, or if we enjoyed a seven-course breakfast concluding at quarter 'til eleven—none of those things matter, because we have established habitual patterns which must be intentionally discarded if we are to alter our actions.

Now, most of these patterns are built on experience,

31

and we have learned that it is to our advantage not to compromise them.

But, tell me, isn't it wonderful when we do?

Have you ever sat smiling as the phone jingled within arm's reach?

Have you ever looked both ways at a deserted intersection and made a left turn against a red light?

And have you ever worked right through the lunch hour with nary a pang of hunger?

I am convinced there is a tiny, two-fisted fighter in the soul of every human being, constantly proclaiming, "Do it your own way. . . . Remember, you are different. . . . Maintain your independence." Most of the time I would applaud the little rascal for bringing the best out of us, but from time to time, that gremlin robs us of hope by demanding we maintain control of every situation. Hope, at its best, calls for a release of control.

That's why Thomas is such a prototype individual for most of us. Perhaps more than any other character in biblical literature, he could slip into our society undetected. We would spot Peter right away; he's too impulsive. And Luke would be equally easy—too studious. And, of course, John would be a snap, with all his gentle characteristics. All those guys would stick out like sore thumbs. But not Thomas. He would fit right in. Intense, hard-driving, in need of acceptance, he was nonetheless a realist whose conditioned responses simply made it impossible for him to accept the rumor of the resurrection. "No way," he protested; "I won't buy it until I feel the wound in his side and the holes in his hands." He was literally hope-less.

PRECONDITIONED FOR DOUBT

Are we so different from Thomas?

Our experience runs directly contrary to the words

we intone every Easter, "Lives again our glorious King, where, O death, is now thy sting?" We have never conversed with one who was dead and buried. We have never clasped the hand of one fresh forth from the tomb. And when we consider the facts about what happens to the human body after death, it is downright ridiculous to suggest decayed tissue, decomposed bone, and an oxygen-starved brain can reunite into a whole and healthy person. We would not believe any claim that the *Challenger Seven* was back at work, so why should we believe this stuff about Christ?

THE EXPERIENCE BLOCK

If experience is our guide, it is no wonder we feel so hopeless.

One of the great faith epics of the Old Testament involves three characters by the names of Shadrach, Meshach, and Abednego. You remember the story: Confronted by the hatred of King Nebuchadnezzar, these three were forced to choose between God and the world. Before thousands of watchers, the king ordered Shadrach, Meshach, and Abednego to denounce their God and kneel before his. Said Nebuchadnezzar, "If you refuse, I'll toss you into a fiery furnace."

For most of us, that would have sealed the deal. We know about fire. We have seen what it can do, and we have felt its fury. On the other hand, as nice as all the theory might be, very few of us claim to know, see, or feel God. Thus, based on our experience, we would avoid the fire and deal with God later.

The difference is a matter of faith.

Shadrach, Meshach, and Abednego had a ton of it.

Refusing to kneel, they were tossed in the furnace, only to emerge unharmed.

It's a great old story. But let's be straight about it—we don't really believe it happened. Even if it did, it couldn't happen to us. Based on simple experience, we believe more in the fury of fire than the faithfulness of God. We would not do what those guys did. We would not trust God against the world. Our experience forbids us that pleasure.

But wait. If experience is our benchmark, then fortune is our God. So long as life is good, we can believe God is good. We can trust. But what happens if life turns sour? What happens when we smack into disaster? What happens when the prognosis stinks and the experts run out of answers?

WHEN HOPE FADES

Perhaps we can catch a clue by looking at Beirut. Just a few years ago it was considered the garden spot of the Middle East. It was the playground of the power people, a harbor for monastic believers, and tourism was its primary source of income.

No more. The luxury hotels are either destroyed or occupied by militiamen. The monasteries are encircled with barbed wire and mine fields. And the only people intentionally visiting are politicians or profiteers bent on taking advantage of a desperate situation.

In the midst of this, Yiha Basal, a veteran militiaman at nineteen years of age, sits down with some friends to play a game. They start with a .357 magnum Ruger pistol. One bullet is placed in the six-chamber cylinder. For thirty seconds or so, the young man sits smiling as he spins the cylinder. Then, calmly, staring straight ahead, he places the muzzle of the pistol against his temple and pulls the trigger.

Though his chances were one in six, Basal blew away the right side of his head.

The game is played daily in Lebanon. They call it the death game. To be sure, these hopeless young men don't even see it as a test of courage. As *Newsweek* magazine explained, it is a test of despair. Life has gone sour, so it doesn't matter any more.

Is it any wonder they can machine-gun airline counters, hijack cruise ships, or drive a dynamite-laden pickup truck into a concrete barricade? When experience is God, such despair is as near as a doctor's diagnosis or a call in the night. When hope is smothered, life is cheap.

THE HOPE–DOUBT PARADOX

But, for the believer, a distant message sounds softly on the ear: "I will not leave you desolate; I will come to you. Yet a little while, and the world will see me no more, but you will see me; because I live, you will live also" (John 14:18-19).

This is the message of hope so desperately needed in our time. But as often as it is repeated, it is still very difficult to accept. On paper, by the numbers, according to the best efforts of the computer and the records of the county coroner, there is no way anybody ever rose from the dead. So let us get in line with Thomas. Let us assume the position of those who simply can't believe because they've never seen.

But even as we step into the realist line, let us be aware of what we are missing.

I doubt there is a better summary statement in all of the Scriptures than that afforded Thomas by the Master. After proof by contact, the Lord turned to the converted skeptic and said, "Have you believed because you have seen me? Blessed are those who have not seen and yet believe."

In other words, the happiest people in the world are those who break their conditioned responses, those who swim upstream.

Blessed are those who sometimes refuse to answer the phone.

Blessed are those who have prudently run a red light.

Blessed are those who eat only when they need it.

And blessed are those who know how to grow against the grain, and hope.

You see, Thomas was one of the lucky ones, and Christ knew it. The doubting disciple had the privilege of physical contact with the risen Lord. His hope was based on firsthand experience. He believed because he *knew*. We must hope because we *trust*, and that is a matter of choice.

THE CHALLENGE OF CHOICE

William Glasser explains that all human behavior is a matter of selected alternatives. He says those people who blame circumstance for making them miserable are completely off-base. Life does not happen to us, we happen to life, and the way we deal with it is entirely up to us. Dr. Glasser writes: "Nothing we do is caused by what happens outside of us. If we believe what we do is caused by forces outside of us, we are acting like dead machines, not living human beings" (*Take Effective Control of Your Life* [New York: Harper & Row, 1984], p. 1).

When the boss walks in and gives us a 20 percent raise, we choose how to respond. When the stock market hits the skids and we lose a fortune in fifteen minutes, we choose how to respond. When the police department calls to announce that a youngster with the same last name as ours has been arrested for shoplifting, we choose how to respond. When the doctor stands somberly beside the bed and mumbles, "There is nothing more we can do," we choose how to respond. When the bank schedules a date to auction the family farm, we choose how to respond. When a dear friend declares, "I have AIDS," we choose how to respond. Ours is the choice to hope or not to hope, no matter what the situation might be.

TRUST AND ACCEPTANCE

These things do not happen *to* us, they happen around us. What we do with them depends in large part on what we believe. Recall again what Christ said to Thomas after their famous encounter: "Do you believe because you have seen? Blessed are those who have not seen and yet believe."

The key word is the one translated "believe." In the Greek it is *pisteuo* and it offers us the root form of several other key words such as trust and acceptance. In fact, it would be fair to define "believing" as the conscious choice to accept trustfully. When we believe in a person we accept that person trustfully. When we believe in a product we buy it trustfully. And when we believe in a doctrine, we embrace it trustfully.

The recent rash of tampering incidents involving over-the-counter drugs reiterates the issue. Until some demented fool contaminated some Tylenol capsules, it was one of the most trustworthy pain remedies in the world. Millions of people chose to believe in it. I suspect most of us have, at one time or another, used it.

Why?

Because we fully understood the ingredients?

Because we had experienced the effects before?

Because we had a computer print-out from Johnson & Johnson?

No way. We consumed the pain reliever because we trusted its maker and accepted testimony from those who had used it before.

The Master looked at hard-thinking Thomas and said what was on his mind. "Sure, Thomas, you believe because you have seen. And that's OK. But the real blessing will come to those who can believe because they trust the Maker and accept the testimony of others."

It's OK to be a little suspicious of Tylenol. After all, it's been proven fallible. But tell me, when was the resurrected Lord so compromised? By what process has the power of Christ been broken by the tampering of humanity? And where is the record indicating the King of Easter has failed to keep his word?

DIVIDED BY CHOICES: THE DOUBLE YELLOW LINE

Ultimately, a faith posture is determined by a one-on-one encounter with Christ. I believe all of us, like Thomas in the Upper Room, are destined for a face-to-face moment with the Lord wherein doubt will be destroyed by undeniable reality. At that time, all will believe even as Thomas believed, because there will be no other choice. But until that moment, we stand on opposite sides of a mythical double yellow line—divided by choice. On one side, by choice, is the Thomas crowd, paralyzed by logic, handcuffed by experience. On the other, also by choice, are the children of hope. With confidence in the Maker and reliance on the assertion of the saints, these are the folk who handle all of life with a degree of triumph and trust. They are not victims of life but victors in life. In the world but not of it, they are, indeed, blessed.

Thus, as we begin our examination of hope, it is appropriate to note the double yellow line between the children of doubt and the children of hope, but only for the sake of definition. Both belong to him. Christ did not say, "Because you couldn't believe without seeing you are condemned, Thomas." All he said was, "Blessed are those who do not see, and yet believe!"

So the real challenge of hope is the challenge of trusting God's promise as revealed in Jesus Christ. "I go to prepare a place for you." That means crossing the double yellow line. It means releasing control. It means claiming a future when there is no light at the end of the tunnel.

AVOIDING JUDGMENT

I have a good friend who claims to be a mechanical moron. He tells of taking a bicycle next door so a neighbor could assemble it on Christmas Eve. As he sat watching his friend construct the bike, guilt got the best of him and he decided he had to do something to help. His eyes focused on the handlebars, neatly set to one side along with the grips, which were equipped with a super-glue adhesive. He thought, "At least I can stick the grips on the handlebars." So he did.

Forty-five minutes later, the major assembly completed, his friend said, "Give me the handlebars, Dick, it's time to slide them through the gooseneck!"

The next morning, my friend's ten-year-old was delighted to find a spanking new bicycle waiting for her. She had just two questions. "Daddy, why is there only one grip on the handlebars? And what is this sticky stuff?"

I believe one of the major causes of hopelessness in our time is a tendency of some believers to put on the grips before the handlebars are in the gooseneck. Specifically, I am referring to the practice of writing off all those who, like Thomas, have trouble believing without seeing. By insisting on rock-hard adherence to creeds, we exclude thousands of folk who just might share a hammock with us in the hereafter.

A TIME OF RECKONING

As I wrap up this first chapter, I want you to consider the truth that Paul so clearly enunciated in the second chapter of his letter to the Philippians, when he observed the day will come when "at the name of Jesus every knee [shall] bow, in heaven and on earth and under the earth, and every tongue confess that Jesus Christ is Lord, to the glory of God" (Philippians 2:6-11).

In other words, the day will come when everybody will cross over the double yellow line. The day will come when every man, every woman, and every child who ever drew a breath will confess Jesus Christ as Lord and enter the kingdom of heaven. Now, I realize this is in direct conflict with the accepted theory that some are destined for eternal bliss and some for eternal torment. I realize it flashes in the face of what many have been taught regarding the need for conversion before death. And I also realize it could be interpreted as a license to sin.

All of those are issues we must confront in the following chapters. Still, the towering message of Christ's victory over death, and the anchor of hope in the face of all despair, is the confidence that the love of God will one day embrace every human being. If a person can trust that truth, no problem is insurmountable.

THE STYLE OF HOPE

The epic of Masada stands as a high-water mark in the annals of Hebrew courage. At the same time, it could be noted as a low-water mark in the record of Hebrew faith. Some of you will recall that Masada is a towering rock fortress on the shore of the Dead Sea, where a handful of Jews bravely endured a siege by overwhelming Roman forces. Ultimately, rather than surrender, they took their own lives.

Some see this as a tremendous act of courage. I have trouble with that. I see suicide as the ultimate step of self-control, the epitome of self turning to self, a denial of the basic Christian conviction that all things work together for good for those who love God and are called according to the Creator's purpose. I don't want to pass judgment on the people at Masada, I just want to underscore the hopelessness of total human control.

To trust in God is to expect the best and leave space for intercession; it is to point to a risen Lord who escaped tomb, boulder, and soldier to prove the power of God over the intent of human beings. It is to ride the waves rather than attempt to calm the sea.

THE ROLE OF PATIENCE

That calls for patience.

In the eighth chapter of his letter to the Romans, verse eight, Paul pinpointed the relationship between patience and hope. He wrote: "Now hope that is seen is not hope. For who hopes for what he sees? But if we hope for what we do not see, we wait for it with patience."

The prophet Isaiah picked up the same theme:

They who wait upon the Lord shall renew their strength,
    they shall mount up with wings like eagles,
they shall run and not be weary,
    they shall walk and not faint.

(Isaiah 40:31)

Both are underlining the truth that God's timetable is not subject to human manipulation. It does not change no matter how much we fret and fume. Hence, the person of peace is the one who can back off the throttle and relax. Choosing hope means taking life's surprises in stride, in the knowledge that "in the fullness of time" everything will be OK.

Back in 1974 the postmaster in a small town in Montana opened a manila envelope from his superiors at the regional headquarters in San Francisco. It was standard operating procedure for them to send a package of pep talks and policy interpretations, the kind of stuff executives plague subordinates with. When he dumped the contents on his desk, he couldn't believe his eyes. Out tumbled two snakes about eighteen inches long, one red, the other blue-gray. They landed on his desk top and started wiggling.

The elderly postmaster did what most people do when surprised by snakes—he screamed and scrambled for safety. His pulse rate quickened, his breathing became heavy, his adrenalin flowed.

Then, as his eyes began to refocus, he noted the snakes had stopped moving. Cautiously, he approached his desk, picked up a ruler, and poked it at the red one. It rolled over with no response. Relieved, he realized the snakes were rubber.

Now he was angry. He grabbed the manila envelope and rifled through its contents, searching for an explanation for this nonsense. At last, he found it, a small typewritten note. It read something like this: "Enclosed are two rubber snakes. We call them 'Hazard Adders.' We see them as a marvelous way to be sure your employees are constantly alert. For best effect, hide them in unexpected places."

The postmaster promptly tossed one note and two "Hazard Adders" into the garbage can.

I share that story at this point because it lifts up an opportunity to underline patience. There are those who believe God works like the Western Regional Office of the United States Postal Service, willing to do anything to rattle our cages and keep us on the alert. As a consequence, these poor folk are forever anticipating the worst, ready to disintegrate at the slightest provocation, so tightly wound they can't sit still for ten minutes, let alone trust the providence of God for the whole of their lives. These are the people who are forever uttering, "Praise The Lord!" through gritted teeth under ice-coated eyes. They may speak of patience but they project an image of rigidly controlled paranoia.

True patience is the capacity to manifest forbearance under the provocation of strain, to hang loose, to laugh in the presence of "Hazard Adders."

BEYOND HUMAN EXPERIENCE

God never promised a life free from trial. What God promised was to be with us always and, through the risen Lord, to give us ultimate victory.

To be sure, Christ will not be bound by human experience.

If we believe Jesus Christ was crucified, died and

was buried, and on the third day rose from the dead, then we obviously accept the fact this was no ordinary human being. Christ had and has powers which exceed human understanding and experience.

This has been the center of Christian hope since that magic moment when Mary of Magdala heard the Master utter her name in the garden outside his tomb. Until that moment, few really knew his power. Since that moment, few can deny it.

ALL–INCLUSIVE

Here I want to make a special point on behalf of those on the Thomas side of the double yellow line. If it was beyond the capacity of those who walked with him (e.g., Mary, Peter, and Thomas) to discern his power, how much more is it beyond the capacity of a twentieth-century citizen to comprehend the authenticity of the Son of God? Still, even though she did not believe Jesus would conquer the grave, Mary was not rejected by him when he did.

That is a very important observation.

Just imagine the scene. The woman came to grieve a dead teacher. She returned praising a risen Lord who loved her in spite of her doubt.

Can you imagine the reversal she experienced? Here she was, burdened with a visit of death. He was gone. Dead. She had watched him die. Without question, her spirit was broken when she entered that garden. When he walked up and asked her, "Woman, why are you weeping? Whom do you seek?" she didn't even recognize him.

So what did he do? He shattered the shell of her human experience with a single utterance—her name: "Mary." And, in that instant, her doubt, her emptiness, her grief, her confusion, and her obvious inability to believe that he was the Son of God vanished. What she, from the midst of her humanity, could not or would not comprehend, Christ, from the midst of his divinity, made unmistakably clear.

If he would do that for her, why do we doubt he would do it for all? If he would call "Mary," what makes us think he will not call "Barry" or "Ruth" or "John" or "Linda"? He knows our names, and in the fullness of time he will call them.

UNCONQUERABLE LOVE

You see, God's love will not be defeated. The crucifixion stands as the human rejection of the truth. "For God so loved the world that he gave his only Son, that whoever believes in him should not perish but have eternal life" (John 3:16). The resurrection is God's response to that rejection. And there's that word again, *believe*. The challenge is to accept trustingly the promise of Christ to draw all humanity to himself.

Our problem in dealing with the idea of ultimate salvation for all humanity centers in underestimating God's love and overestimating our experience. And at the center of the issue is our conception of time.

Because our experience is bounded by birth on one end and death on the other, we assume the right to limit God's work to the same arena. In doing so, we put the grips on the handlebars before inserting them in the gooseneck. We make an assumption to which we have no right.

THE TIME LINE

We are correct in measuring our actions on the time line between birth and death. That's where we live.

But we are tragically incorrect when we try to limit God's actions to our experience. On what basis do we assume that an encounter with Christ after death will be any less valid than such an encounter in the present?

I find it interesting that the very folk who would reject the concept of ultimate inclusive salvation are the same folk who pronounce humanism the great enemy of the faith. Yet, I would ask, is there any stronger humanism than that which forces God to work on a human timetable? So confined, Jesus Christ would have never escaped the tomb.

So our hope hinges on God's power to work within and without the parameters of time as we know it. One day, I believe, every human being will come face to face with our Lord and, beholding his unconditional love, not one will deny him.

Paul said it: "Lo! I tell you a mystery. We shall not all sleep, but we shall all be changed, in a moment, in the twinkling of an eye, at the last trumpet. For the trumpet will sound, and the dead will be raised imperishable, and we shall be changed" (I Corinthians 15:51-52).

This is the center of a hope which is unconquerable. Ultimately, Jesus Christ will prove totally victorious. Our actions, no matter how sinful, no matter how foolish, cannot scuttle God's plan to fellowship forever with us.

THE CALL FOR RESPONSIBILITY

I recall sharing this concept of salvation with a group of college students in Murfreesboro, Tennessee. Immediately, one of them snapped, "That is really super! Now I can do anything I feel like doing without worrying about the consequences."

Wrong. There is nothing more demanding than

love, and furthermore, to be unconditionally loved does not mean we will not be held accountable for our actions. Suggesting that there is no eternal condemnation is not the same as suggesting that there will be no judgment and no punishment for disobedience to God.

No one makes a more eloquent explanation of this point than Madeleine L'Engle in *The Irrational Season*.

I know a number of highly sensitive and intelligent people in my own communion who consider as a heresy my faith that God's loving concern for his creation will outlast all of our willfulness and pride. No matter how many eons it takes, he will not rest until all of creation, including Satan, is reconciled to him, until there is no creature who cannot return his look of love with a joyful response of love.

Origen held this belief and was ultimately pronounced a heretic. Gregory of Nyssa, affirming the same loving God, was made a saint. Some people feel it to be heresy because it appears to deny man his freedom to refuse to love God. But this, it seems to me, denies God his freedom to go on loving us beyond all our willfulness and pride. If the Word of God is the light of the world, and this light cannot be put out, ultimately it will brighten all the dark corners of our hearts and we will be able to see, and seeing, will be given the grace to respond with love . . . and of our own free will.

The church has always taught that we will pay for our sins, that we shall be judged and punished according to our sinfulness. But I cannot believe that God wants punishment to go on interminably any more than does a loving parent. The entire purpose of loving punishment is to teach, and it lasts only as long as is needed for the lesson. And the lesson is always love. ([New York: Seabury, 1979] p. 96)

Hence, the foundation for our hope is clear. God loves us more than we can mess up. Furthermore, God wants us to return that love, not for fear of hell but because God first loved us. In my opinion, love shies to root in fear but flourishes magnificently in simple trust. Crossing the double yellow line between doubt and total confidence is an ongoing process. Some days it will be easier than others. There will be times when there is virtually no doubt in your mind but that God is totally involved with your journey. There will be others when such certainty will seem light-years in the distance. Both can be times of hope.

CLAIMING A FUTURE

Alan Walker shares the incident with which I wish to conclude this chapter. It deals with a young woman for whom crossing the double yellow line seemed impossible. Vicki was raised in the church, a veteran of Sunday school, confirmation class, youth fellowship, and the high school choir. She was a beautiful girl with flowing blond hair, sparkling blue eyes, and a quick, effervescent smile.

Somehow, she drifted away from her roots and got tangled up with drugs.

Walker says he noticed her eyes first. The twinkle was gone. In its place was a drab, sullen emptiness. Next, her attitude shifted. Enthusiasm gave way to cynicism, joy to gloom, confidence to criticism. As her problem increased, her voice thickened, her skin discolored, and her eyes took on a permanent glaze. Counselors agreed, apart from a dramatic change, she would be dead before her twenty-fifth birthday. Writes Walker:

Recently, Vicki stood before the television cameras in a worship service televised from Sydney, Australia, and quietly told her story. "I knew the Christian message, but for years I rejected Christ. Then one day in desperation I said, 'God, why don't you come close to me?' He replied, 'Vicki, I cannot come any closer to you, I am with you now.'

Suddenly I was overcome with the thought of God's infinite patience. Even though I had rejected him a hundred times yet he was with me still. And at that moment I accepted Jesus Christ. Look, I am free." And she was. Now her eyes were clear, her voice strong, her skin clear. Vicki now had a future. ("The Easter People," in *The Miracle of Easter*, Floyd Thatcher, ed. [Waco, Tx.: Word, 1980], p. 112)

Is that not the essence of hope, to have a future?

2

The Foundations of Hope

THE PHOTO ALBUM THEORY

Of all the insights I have gathered from William Glasser, I question if any is more helpful than that of being "picture driven." The California psychologist makes a great case for what prompts human behavior. He explains that each of us has a mental photo album filled with appropriate images. Our behavior stems from attempting to satisfy these images. There's one for relaxation (the beach, the golf course, a fishing boat). There's one for power (blue pinstriped suits, corner offices, multiple assistants). There's one for family (spouse, two children, holiday gatherings). And there's one for church (big building, organ music, sermons). Now, if you found yourself disagreeing with the pictures I have suggested, I have already made my point. No two people carry the same photo albums. Hence, interpersonal behavior is a matter of constantly negotiating unmatched images.

In this chapter my purpose is to set before you the images that give foundation to my hope. Neither of us should expect total concurrence. However, if my images prompt a reevaluation of yours, this book is doing both of us a favor.

Three concepts combine to give credence to my hope: first, the resurrection of Jesus Christ; second, an awareness of human sin; and third, justification by grace.

THE POWER OF GOD

I fled Him, down the nights and down the days;
  I fled Him, down the arches of the years;
I fled Him, down the labyrinthine ways
  Of my own mind; and in the mist of tears
I hid from Him, and under running laughter.
    Up vistaed hopes, I sped;
    And shot, precipitated,
Adown Titanic glooms of chasmed fears,
  From those strong Feet that followed, followed after.
    But with unhurrying chase,
    And unperturbed pace,
  Deliberate speed, majestic instancy,
    They beat—and a Voice beat
    More instant than the Feet—
  "All things betray thee, who betrayest Me."
          (Francis Thompson, "The Hound of Heaven")

The truth that we must claim if we are to fathom the meaning of hope is that our deeds (good or bad) can never daunt the purpose of God. The issue is not our coming to God. It is God's coming to us. We are not dealing with our power, but with that of the Author of life. Our hope is centered not in our ability to learn how to handle things but in the fact that God has never ceased to manage life.

The prophet Isaiah underlined this truth when he wrote,

The Lord of hosts has sworn:
"As I have planned,
  so shall it be,
and as I have purposed,
  so shall it stand."

(Isaiah 14:24)

Any understanding of hope will be strengthened if it begins with the acknowledgment of the omnipotence of the Almighty. God is in charge.

The issue is not our coming to God, it is God's coming to us.

In voluntarily assuming the form of a man, God expressed to all humanity the heighth, depth, and breadth of a power that cannot be denied, no matter what we do. It is the power of light over darkness, of joy over despair, of life over death. It is the power of hope.

THE POWER OF HIS PRESENCE

Through the incarnation, God offers a new level of understanding to all of us. Not only are we privileged to live in a model manner, we are also exposed to a touch of reassurance about eternity. If the Creator can divinely enter life in the person of Jesus Christ, why do we find it so difficult to believe death cannot be conquered at the same time?

Snuggled in the deft phrases of the prologue to the Gospel of John are profound truths reaching far beyond the common perimeters of contemporary Christianity. Here, John tells us, the power of God preexisted all life as we know it: "In the beginning was the Word, and the Word was with God, and the Word was God." This power was made available and vulnerable in the person of Jesus Christ: "And the Word became flesh and dwelt among us"; "He was in

53

the world, and the world was made through him, yet the world knew him not. He came to his own home and his own people received him not." In spite of this rejection, the power of God prevailed and will prevail through all eternity: "The light shines in the darkness, and the darkness has not overcome it" (John 1:1-4).

That power stands at the heart of our hope. We have a future because God claimed it for us two thousand years ago.

POWER IN PAIN

As a child of hope I make it a point to remember such power whenever misfortune befalls me. I can never be invulnerable to pain or tragedy, but with an image of the power of God in my mental photo album I can stand boldly in the face of disaster. I will still feel pain. I will still feel loneliness. I will still feel disappointment. I will not feel defeated, for my hope is not confined to the present.

I believe this is what Paul was highlighting when he said to the Corinthians, "For [Christ] was crucified in weakness, but lives by the power of God."

As a man, the Lord could be humiliated, tortured, and killed. But as a child of God, he was invincible, above it all, conqueror of the grave, a true manifestation of the power of God. Hence, any understanding of the life of Jesus Christ must start with the power of God. And that power, like all true power, is made perfect in vulnerability.

THE STRENGTH OF VULNERABILITY

"Kai o logos sarx egeneto, kai eskenosen en umin." "And the Word became flesh and dwelt among us."

That phrase underscores God's commitment to all humanity. It is the pivot point of our hope. I provide the Greek text because it highlights an essential part of my photo album.

The key word here is *eskenosen,* translated "dwelt." Actually, it has a great deal more meaning than that. Its root is the word *sknvn,* which means "tent." Literally translated, it means God "pitched his tent with us." God made Christ available as a matter of free will. We didn't hire him. We didn't entice him. We didn't give him a scholarship and laundry money. God, in Christ, was a "walk on."

There is no more power than this. Those present on a voluntary basis can leave at any time. Present because they choose to be, they have unequivocal possession of control. And when, subject to abuse, they stick around anyway, their power is increased proportionately.

I have a friend in Chicago who immersed himself in the prison ministry in Illinois. Even though he was serving a church at the time, he gave thirty or forty hours a week to visiting prisons, relating to convicts, writing letters to those on the inside, and finding jobs for those on the outside. His was a ministry of "being there" no matter the cost. Sometimes it wasn't appreciated. He was spit upon, cursed, often threatened with murder. Still, he kept going back.

Then the state got word of the task he was doing, and the governor's office called him in and offered him a job as the head chaplain for the whole system. Flattered and fascinated, he went to the United Methodist bishop to ask for a special appointment to accept the invitation. He was shocked when his boss said, "Bill, you don't want that job!" "Why not?" he asked. "Because," said the bishop, "as soon as you go on the payroll, your ministry is compromised; you become one with The Man."

Bill refused the job.

THERE TO CARE

There is quite a difference between caring for someone because it's part of your job and caring from the heart. Any up-front minister can tell you that. By the book, a minister loves all the people in the church. But, take my word for it, there is a difference between those one loves because it's in the job description and those one loves because it's in the heart.

When God became man in the person of Jesus Christ, there were no strings attached. This is the picture that most allows me to be hopeful in all situations, no matter who is involved.

If, indeed, "the Word was with God, and the Word was God," he had nothing to gain by enduring the indignities of humanity. Nevertheless, he "pitched his tent with us" so as to show us the power of God's love in life, over death.

Could there be a better foundation for our hope? Consider the two primary ingredients; God's love and God's power. Both have been undeniably demonstrated in the life, death, and resurrection. For whom?

And we should ever be hopeless?

TAMPERING WITH A GOOD THING

Ah, but the fact that God never stops caring about us does not mean we will care for God in return. In fact, we are much more apt to deny God's power than we are to embrace it. We have a sad tendency to be hope-less on our own rather than hope-filled with the

Master. Why? Because we are inordinately self-centered.

I had a friend who killed himself. Not abruptly, but slowly, over a period of time. I knew he was doing it. He knew he was doing it. I could do nothing about it. He would do nothing about it.

We tried but we failed.

Within a week of my arrival in that community I dropped in at his store to make a purchase. He told me he was a part of my flock and asked if I would join him for lunch. I did and the friendship was born. Don was cordial, articulate, dapper, and successful. In his mid-fifties, he had built a nice business, solid enough that his sons were now calling the shots, secure in the commercial kingdom Dad had constructed. He came to the store just long enough to check the mail. Then he was off to drink lunch.

That first day, I watched him nail four Manhattans and knew he had a problem. It took several months before the issue was touched. When I finally brought it up, Don seemed grateful. We talked about treatment and enrolled him in the best alcoholic rehabilitation center in the area. He was there for a month. Our first lunch afterward was a celebration, a dry celebration. He talked freely about his condition, appearing to be on top of it.

Six months later, out to lunch with someone else, I spotted Don sitting alone at a corner table—Manhattan equipped. He smiled as I approached the table. "Don't say anything, Barry, I know what I'm doing. I can handle it now."

He lasted two years.

TURN, TURN, TURN

Paul Tillich defines sin as "the turning of the self to the self." Alcoholism underscores the power of this definition. People cursed by this terrible disease stand as classic illustrations of the manner in which the self inexorably fails the self. But, lest the rest of us feel smug in the shadow of such a condition, let us be quick to observe that alcoholism only confirms a condition common to us all. There is no such thing as a totally self-sufficient human being.

The prudent alcoholic accepts that truth and overcomes the self by centering elsewhere. The prudent Christian, in search of hope, does the same thing. So long as we are dependent on our own power, we are destined to one day be hopeless. Even if we can afford limitless luxury, the day still comes when we cannot purchase an escape from reality, when we must deal with our mortality. Then, our only hope is in a strength far beyond ourselves.

You may wonder why I would choose to introduce the subject of sin into an analysis of human hope. I found it unavoidable. I believe it is virtually impossible for us to live without sinning. Thus, if we are to manifest hope, we must do so from the midst of sin. "For I do not do what I want, but I do the very thing I hate" (Romans 7:15).

EASY TO UNDERSTAND, AWESOME TO OVERCOME

Unlike the resurrection, sin is easy for us to understand. It is simple.

It is not by accident the narrative of the original sin centers in the chomp of an apple. So easy. So commonplace. So natural. Still, it is not the deed which is disastrous. It is the motive. Anytime the human will takes precedence over the divine will, the consequence is sin.

The biblical record says God warned man and

woman not to eat of the tree of the knowledge of good and evil. The symbolism here is vivid. It's not the hands or the teeth or the tongue which corrupt. It is the head and the heart. Knowledge is the issue. Once we think we can do as we please, once we discover the freedom of the will, we have made contact with the web of sin.

I think of a mother and child sunning at the beach. The mother knows the danger of the water, the treachery of the current, the power of the waves. Hence she instructs her beloved, "Don't go near the water." Then she stretches out in the sun and closes her eyes.

Now, the emerging will of the wee one surfaces. "Mom's not looking. I can dig in the sand. I can build a sand castle. I can feed our picnic lunch to the seagulls. But, can I go in the water?" And the circle of play grows and grows until, one eye on Mom, the child plunks the first toe in the water. "Yes! No matter what Mom says, I CAN GO IN THE WATER!"

From that moment on, the water is no longer the issue. The self has turned to the self. Personal will has exceeded parental will. The "I," indifferent to all but itself, has arrived.

Sin is simple. It is the "I" above all else.

It is also the single greatest barrier between despair and hope. Caught up in myself, I cannot be hopeful because I am all too aware of my frailty, my brokenness, my weakness.

Jacques Ellul describes the dilemma this way:

The moment I am aware of myself I become the unique, central, and essential person who lies behind everything. Only my own destiny concerns me. For I am the central thing in the world. We thus see the dawn of pride, egoism, and also of worry and anxiety. For if the self is the center of all things, if everything begins with me, then how can I avoid the anguished realization that everything also ends with me? (*The Ethics of Freedom*, p. 136)

Such is the blindness of sin. And tragically, the more successful a person becomes, the more overwhelming is the problem. If the child who managed to get one toe in the water is heady with freedom, how much more so is the business magnate who can buy and sell whatever she pleases, or the starlet with legions kneeling at her feet, or the politician in command of thousands of patronage positions, or the preacher called to lead four thousand believers?

THE DOMINANT INTEREST

Paul was wrestling with this truth when he wrote to the Philippians: "Do nothing from selfishness or conceit, but in humility count others better than yourselves. Let each of you look not only to his own interests, but also to the interests of others" (Philippians 2:3-4).

Whatever else, we must be saved from believing "we did it on our own."

The word the apostle used for "conceit" sheds more light on the concept of sin: *Kenodoxos* means "hollow."

When I think of hollow persons, some new pictures pop up from my photo album.

First, I see the person who is always intentionally groomed. Mind you, I'm not taking a shot at good grooming. I'm taking a shot at good grooming as a cover-up. These people have to look good on the surface because that's as deep as they get. The issue is to shape an image void of internal investment. If the hollow person can keep us concerned about colors, textures, and designs, we may never get to the concepts of integrity, loyalty, and depth.

Second, I see the person whose vocabulary is intentionally vague. Hollow people are genuises when it comes to saying exciting things that can't be pinned down. They promise support, but fail to show up. They express concern, but flee from action. They specialize in smoke and avoid all fire.

And finally, the hollow person always wants credit for everything done. These are the folk who seek seats in high places, acknowledgments in print, and special awards at the annual banquet. They want thank-you notes for their annual pledge and their names listed in the church bulletin. Self so centered in self, the hollow person is forever on the take. And they've been around a long time. Remember these words: "Woe to you, scribes and Pharisees, hypocrites! for you are like whitewashed tombs, which outwardly appear beautiful, but within they are full of dead men's bones and all uncleanness. So you also outwardly appear righteous to men, but within you are full of hypocrisy and iniquity" (Matthew 23:27-28).

In the midst of this self-centered hollowness there is a final ingredient of sin which directly conflicts with the concept of hope. Having scrambled to create a kingdom for the self, the hollow person lives in constant *fear* of losing that kingdom.

FEAR OF FALLING

Is there a more formidable barrier to hope than fear?

Aaron Stern, whose analysis of the influence of narcissism in America is a classic, in my opinion, observes: "The more narcissistic [self centered] among us are always just around the corner from their next depression."

Isn't it the truth? When the whole world is seen as a personal pacifier, the slightest rejection crushes the spirit and paralyzes the psyche. Now do you understand why I felt it necessary to deal with sin in a book about hope? If anything prevents us from practicing hope, it is the nearsighted notion that the future depends on us; it is the farfetched dream that we are in charge of tomorrow; it is the nagging consciousness that we are unable to cope with today, let alone tomorrow.

I think of the Valium-vacuumed housewife who sat petrified in my office many years ago, telling a story about everything leading to nothing. Her closets were full. Her car was new. Her house was immense. Her yard was immaculate. Her figure was superb. *And her soul was empty.* A veteran of twenty years in the image-conscious suburbs, she was as self-centered a hollow human being as I have ever met. And she was trembling with fear.

Why? Because when the trimmings were pressed to the side, she knew herself. All the external paraphernalia simply camouflaged the internal echo chamber and she knew it. She was petrified at being found out.

The next time she came in, I suggested we take a ride. She agreed, and we drove directly to a mental hospital. Her eyes widened as we approached the main entrance. She was so hopeless she thought I was attempting to get her admitted. When I introduced her to the administrator and asked for a tour of the facility, she started to lighten up. Within a few weeks, she was going there daily—not as a patient, but as a volunteer. She virtually rediscovered herself by getting outside herself. She read stories, played checkers, led walks, and shared prayers with the patients.

Later, when her husband lost his job and their fast paced life-style shifted into low gear, she was the steady one who held him together until he found another job. It was no surprise to me. As soon as she quit worrying about losing the veneer of success, she began to lay claim to the heart of success. I can only salute the timeless observation of a friend of mine, "He who finds his life will lose it, and he who loses his life for my sake will find it."

SERVICE THERAPY

If hope seems beyond your grasp, step back and measure where the blocks are. Consider involving yourself in something totally centered in others. Take a look at what you do with your spare time and ponder investing it in some kind of service project.

When I arrived at First Community Church, a fellow by the name of Kenny Krouse took me on as his service project. I didn't know it at the time but he figured I would need all the help I could get to meet the challenge of this ecclesiastical dinosaur. He would stop by the office, call me for lunch, and occasionally drop me a note of encouragement. Our friendship was rudely cut off by Kenny's death just a little over a year later. In the meantime, I learned a great deal from this special man. On one occasion, when I was locked in despair over some issue, he explained how he dealt with depression. "I go to the convalarium," he announced, referring to the hospital wing of First Community Village. "Yep. I go in there and sit down and talk with people who can't see or can't walk or can't even move. And they're always so happy that I stopped by. Every time I come away feeling good about myself and ready to deal with anything."

WHAT PRICE WINNING?

There is a touch of irony here for those whom God has most obviously blessed. People of wealth, people of power, people of influence find it hard to recognize how much fear influences their existence. But it shows up clearly, particularly when they get involved with competition. Every encounter is seen as a win-lose situation. Someone has to come out on top, and power people, accustomed to an elevated view, can be trusted to do everything in their power to win every time. Hence the obsession with being Number One, grabbing the limelight, dumping losers, and worshiping winners. Why? Could it be we are all too aware of our clay feet? Could it be we sense we don't deserve what we have, yet dread the thought of having what we deserve? Could it be that the "mirror, mirror, on the wall" most certainly does know who is fairest of all—and so do we, and it isn't us?

The pungent observation of Paul Tournier comes to mind.

The strong have learned how to play their hand so as to win in the game of life, and they become prisoners of the game. If we are to be strong we must also simplify life, shutting our eyes to its disturbing complexity. Thus the strong quickly become the prisoners of a systematizing habit of mind and a simplistic philosophy which ends by drying them up and cutting them off from true life. (*The Strong and the Weak* [Philadelphia: Westminster, 1963], p. 169)

Claiming hope is first of all a process of overcoming sin. When the apostle Paul would attempt to explain sin, he most often did so in terms of the "flesh" and the "spirit." If one was of the "flesh," it meant the self was completely caught up in itself. On the other hand, if one was of the "spirit," it meant the self had come to terms with its finite condition and surrendered to the will of God.

CHRIST'S ACTION, GOD'S RESPONSE

At Calvary, Jesus Christ totally denied himself. The resurrection is God's answer to that self-denial. Thus, when the self is denied, despair is met with hope. In effect, God said, "When you put yourself down, I will lift you up!"

Theologically, what I am writing about is *justification by grace*. Few doctrines are more important to those who would choose hope. In concluding this chapter on the foundations of hope, I would like to share some thoughts about Martin Luther's favorite concept.

"Take typing"—that might be the most prudent counsel a high school student could receive today. Our world is fast falling under the spell of the computer, to which the doorway is the keyboard.

A few months ago I purchased a word processor. It was a natural acquisition for one whose livelihood depends on the proper alignment of words. At first, I was intimidated by the machine and spent a lot of time talking to strangers in Dallas via a company-supplied toll free number for emergency dilemmas. Within two days, we were on a first name basis. I would call and the switchboard operator would relay my ignorance to the problem solvers: "Barry is on line six; he can't stop the repeating exclamation point."

It was a humiliating experience, but it didn't last long, and now I can't imagine writing anything without my trusty word processor. It lets me change words, relocate paragraphs, correct spelling, alpha-betize lists, and completely remove poorly written pages. I'm fascinated by the thing and few of its talents captivate me more than the justification function.

I've long been a stickler for aesthetics. I like things in balance, visually, and it has always bothered me that I couldn't type to the same specifications that typesetters use for books. I'm sure you've noticed that good books have straight margins on both sides of the page. It doesn't happen by accident. Before the computer, some faithful craftsperson systematically set the type so the right margin was as straight as the left. It was an art, and the average typewriter wouldn't do it.

The word processor does it all. You type a manuscript and punch the "justify" button and sit there and watch words jump all over a screen until they are in perfect alignment. It doesn't change what has been written; it just cleans it up, makes it right, justifies it.

According to Paul, God has been involved with the same process for centuries.

> For we ourselves were once foolish, disobedient, led astray, slaves to various passions and pleasures, passing our days in malice and envy, hated by men and hating one another; but when the goodness and loving kindness of God our Savior appeared, he saved us, not because of deeds done by us in righteousness, but in virtue of his own mercy, by the washing of regeneration and renewal in the Holy Spirit, which he poured out upon us richly through Jesus Christ our Savior, so that we might be justified by his grace and become heirs in hope of eternal life. (Titus 3:3-7)

What does it mean to be "justified by his grace"?

REACHING THE MARK

Pondering that question I am reminded of our goal-oriented society. It seems that every invigorating person is on some kind of predetermined track to glory, for example, lose twenty pounds in sixty days, become a company vice-president within five years, win the club championship in tennis, bridge, golf, or racquetball. And, of course, there's the increasingly ancient but still admirable challenge of becoming a millionaire. This is a nation of achievers, people who set goals and get there!

Still, there is one goal constantly eluding our grasp. Try as we might, we cannot, on our own strength, get right with God! You can't get there from here.

This is the primary issue to which the book of Titus is addressed. There was a powerful group of goal-setting intellectual achievers dominating the religious scene at that time. The Gnostics believed two things were eternal, God and matter. The first was good, the second evil. Hence when God created the world, the Creator did so through a series of emanations that shielded God from corruption through contact with evil matter. Each one of these emanations was more and more distant from God until, at last, they were far enough away for the wicked world to be created.

The challenge, then, for occupants of the earth seeking to communicate and get right with God was to successfully *think* their way through all this interference, back to the Creator. It was a matter of intellectual dexterity. In Gnosticism, we find the most advanced form of "Dungeons and Dragons" ever conceived. The people with the answers had all the advantages. The intellectuals were the ruling class. They shared virtual "passwords," which were believed to get them from one emanation to the next. It was a snobbish system of cerebral isolationism.

Paul looked at this and said, "No way!" If humans can be put right with God via the development of their minds, according to individual effort and social position, then God is not God. Under such a system, the Creator is but the social director at an eternal country club.

It simply cannot work that way. We are put right

with God not through anything that we do but through what God has done already in the person and work of Jesus Christ. We are justified by his grace.

When I hit the "justification" button on my word processor, a power far beyond me takes over and correctly aligns the words in front of me. I don't do it. I don't know how, and furthermore, I don't have the power. The machine does.

In a like manner, we do not have the wisdom or energy to restore our relationship with God. But Christ does. And when God allowed the "Word to become flesh and dwell among us" the button was punched starting the process by which every human being is made right with God.

The Swiss theologian Emil Brunner sums up the logic of this observation: "God alone is good and that alone is good which God does."

A TIMELESS INHERITANCE

Here we pick up a special phrase that tells us about our position in relation to God. Paul says God poured out his Holy Spirit upon us through Jesus Christ so "we might be justified by his grace and become heirs in hope of eternal life."

I like that concept, *heirs in hope.*

Let me ask, Does an heir do anything to deserve the inheritance? Of course not—inheritance is not a matter of *what* you are, it is a matter of *who* you are!

And we, every one of us, are the children of God. So what's the thrust of all this? It's simple. We are just, because God acted in Christ!

Consider the truth in this splendid little analogy drawn from the riches of a lazy Sunday afternoon. You know the scene: NFL on the tube, embers in the fireplace, newspaper all over the family room floor,

Daddy asleep on the couch. Into the room comes a four-year-old. He walks directly to the couch, grabs Daddy's shirttail and yanks on it. Dad rolls over, groggy.

"What do you want?"

"I wanna play."

"Well, Daddy's taking a nap now, maybe we'll play later."

"I wanna play . . . NOW!"

"Aw, gimme a break, son, I'm pooped!"

Tears and screams, "You never want to play with me!"

By this point, Dad is sitting on the edge of the couch, head in hands, trying to figure out what to do. Voila! He spots the newspaper all over the floor and, on one page, a map of the world. Instantly, his genius surges from slumber.

He snatches up the world map and leads the child to the kitchen where he proceeds to cut the map into twenty or thirty jigsaw-type pieces.

"There you go, son, now you can put the world back together."

Convinced he has occupied the lad for at least an hour, he returns to the couch and snuggles in for some more sleep.

Five minutes pass and the shirttail is yanked again. Startled, he rolls over.

"You can't have the world together already!"

"Come and see."

He staggers to the kitchen and, sure enough, there is the world in perfect order.

Dumbfounded, the father stares at his little boy—a chip-off-the-old-block genius.

"How did you do that?"

With a shrug, the boy answers. "It was easy. There

was a picture of some people on the other side and when I got them together right, the world was right!"

Lebanon, El Salvador, Nicaragua, the Philippines, Peking, Moscow, London, Washington, Libya, Columbus—all messed up. All in need of justification. All in need of hope.

For we ourselves were once foolish, disobedient, led astray, slaves to various passions and pleasures, passing our days in malice and envy, hated by men and hating one another, but when the goodness and loving kindness of God our Savior appeared, he saved us, not because of deeds done by us in righteousness, but in virtue of his own mercy, by the washing of regeneration and renewal in the Holy Spirit, which he poured out upon us richly through Jesus Christ our Savior, so that we might be justified by his grace and become heirs in hope of eternal life. The saying is sure. (Titus 3:3-7)

Because we are justified by grace, our sin is overcome and we are free to hope.

3

A Paradigm of Hope

A MATTER OF POSITION

Hope lives between the now and the not yet. It is a point of natural tension, a place where reality intersects with expectation, a place where dreams linger and fear, as we noted in the last chapter, tries to control. To be hopeless is to choose to avoid the tension; to play it safe, if miserable, for the sake of peace of mind. To be hopeful is to willingly embrace the unknown, tackle the questions, and wait for the consequences.

Where will you be in a week? A month? Six months? Six years? Most of us have ideas, none certainty. That's where the tension develops. Yesterday we examined and second-guessed with twenty-twenty hindsight. Today, we can measure and control through paralysis by analysis. But tomorrow is always a matter of speculation, manageable only to the point where life unfolds as expected. How often does that happen?

Robert Grudin, in *Time and the Art of Living*, does a masterful job of clarifying the point I am making. He writes:

Fast drivers can see no further than slow drivers, but they must look further down the road to time their reactions safely. Similarly, people with great projects afoot habitually look further and more clearly into the future than people who are mired in day-to-day concerns. These former control the future because by necessity they must project themselves into it; and the upshot is that, like ambitious settlers, they stake out larger plots and homesteads of time than the rest of us. They do not easily grow sad or old; they are seldom intimidated by the alarms and confusions of the present because they have something greater of their own, some sense of their large and coherent motion in time, to compare with the present. ([San Francisco: Harper & Row, 1982] p. 6)

People of hope always seem to have great projects afoot. With a boundless confidence in the future, they have a tendency to wring the very most out of today, planning, tasting, touching, reaching, growing. They seem to know where they are going. I believe that is what Grudin is underlining here, the difference between knowing one's destination and riding on the wind, the difference between purpose and no purpose, the difference between personal wholeness and circumstantial schizophrenia.

In this chapter I want to direct your attention to the gap between what we are on the inside and what we do on the outside. Then, I intend to illustrate how a point of focus, hope, narrows that gap.

SUSPENDED IN TIME

Several years ago I found myself riding on an Amtrak train through central Illinois. As dusk fell an eerie condition developed. There came a point where the light outside the train was approximately the same intensity as that on the inside. Suddenly, I was aware of the gray silhouettes flashing by on the outside and the concurrent motionless interior of the railroad car as it was reflected in my window. I was the only passenger, and I remember the subtle impact of realizing that this was a picture of human existence: outside awhirl with action and issues, inside predictably ordered and apparently unable or unwilling to interact. I sensed anew the power of the fisherman's prayer, "O Lord, the sea is so great and my boat is so small."

Consider with me the issues currently dominating our newspapers: terrorist atrocities in Lebanon, war in Central America, enough nuclear warheads to obliterate civilization, atmospheric mutation, unemployment, runaway deficits—the list goes on and on. To the average citizen it looks like an impossible, unconquerable morass. The sea seems so great and our boats so small. Under such circumstances, to hope seems ludicrously naïve.

Still, our concurrent prosperity poses a paradox. Has there ever been a time when we had more to enjoy or more to fear? Has there ever been greater tension between outward security and inward uneasiness? Has there ever been a more striking variance between where we stand and what we feel? Has there ever been a greater need or more testing condition for hope?

What we need is some way to create harmony between the chaos on the outside and the hunger for serenity on the inside.

Perhaps we can find strength in Paul's words to the church at Rome.

We know that in everything God works for good with those who love him, who are called according to his purpose. For those whom he foreknew he also predestined to be conformed to the image of his Son, in order that he might be the first-born among many brethren. And those whom he predestined he also called; and those whom he called he also justified; and those whom he justified he also glorified.

What then shall we say to this? If God is for us, who is against us? (Romans 8:28-31)

You see, Paul knew how to strike a balance between outward experience and inward feeling. He knew how to make us maximally effective in a confusing and corrupt world. He knew how to allow us the luxury of hope amid rampant anxiety. He did it by giving us a glimpse of a bigger picture.

Through Jesus Christ we are given a new point of focus. When we center in him and his promise of eternity, we are delivered to calmly endure and carefully encounter life in the whirlwind. In Christ we see ourselves free. Once free, we can hope. And once we hope, we are no longer subject to the numbing influence of the world around us. We live in it. We work in it. We plan in it. We build in it. But we are never controlled by it.

"For freedom Christ has set us free," Paul told the Galatians; "stand fast therefore and do not submit again to a yoke of slavery" (Galatians 5:1).

THE VIEW FROM THE OUTSIDE

I think of the first time I saw my golf swing. I was reminded that what we do and what we think we do are seldom the same. Some guy was using a home video unit on the practice tee and took the liberty to tape a Johnson three-wood shot. Horrible! Too jerky. Too fast. Absolutely wrong.

Yet, what I felt as I hit that shot was poetry in motion. I thought the rhythm was fine, the set up perfect, and the take-away smooth. I needed to get outside myself to properly understand myself.

The First Community television ministry affords me the same process of evaluation. Week after week, as I watch myself preach, I squirm in the knowledge that it can always be done better, that I rarely communicate fully, that there is always room to grow.

In Christ, we get outside ourselves to better understand ourselves. By centering in him we gain a new perspective on ourselves and on life in general. "Because He lives, we shall live also." Knowing that for the future, we are filled with hope in the present. Such knowledge allows us to drive fast. It encourages us to look far down the road and enjoy the journey.

You see, all of us are in motion. We may think we are not changing, but we are. We may think we are not moving, but we are. We may think we have plateaued, but we have not.

I like the way Harvey Cox explains this point as he reflects in his autobiography on the annual experience of witnessing graduation exercises. Note the hope in his feelings.

I am slapped in the face every spring by the irrestistible transiency of life. Caps and gowns always make me sniffle. I also know, however, that such a community is only a more graphic example of the primal fact of human transiency. . . . With or without our compliance the journey limps on. New faces and new situations intrude and upset us, and sometimes gladden us despite our preference for what has been. Not to decide is to decide, and "not to journey is to journey anyway"; so in the long run it is better to be a purposeful traveler, choosing our routes as much as we can, than to be a hog-tied hostage dragged along by forces we cannot influence. (*Just as I Am* [Nashville: Abingdon, 1983], p. 21)

"It is better to be a purposeful traveler . . . "

What is a purposeful traveler if not one filled with hope about a future destination?

Are you a purposeful traveler? Do you know where you're going? Is the beat of hope so strong in your mind that it pulls you into the future?

THE CORE OF OUR HOPE

In the tenth chapter of Matthew there is a beautiful scene involving some purposeful travelers. The Master has assembled an unlikely hodgepodge of characters to be known as disciples, and he is briefing them on the mission to come. He does not mince words. He tells it straight:

Behold, I send you out as sheep in the midst of wolves; so be wise as serpents and innocent as doves. Beware of men; for they will deliver you up to councils, and flog you in their synagogues, and you will be dragged before governors and kings for my sake, to bear testimony before them and the Gentiles. (Matthew 10:16-18)

Imagine the terror that must have filled their hearts. These were ordinary citizens; fishermen, lawyers, doctors, and bookkeepers, people like you and me. But Christ sensed their anxiety and put it to rest by underlining the love and purpose of God. He gave them a point of focus, knowing it would set them free.

Have no fear of [these things]; for nothing is covered that will not be revealed, or hidden that will not be known. What I tell you in the dark, utter in the light; and what you hear whispered, proclaim upon the housetops. And do not fear those who kill the body but cannot kill the soul; rather fear him who can destroy both soul and body in hell. Are not two sparrows sold for a penny? And not one of them will fall to the ground without your Father's will. But even the hairs of your head are all numbered. (Matthew 10:26-30)

The core of our hope is God's unfailing concern for us. Even when it appears we have been forsaken, we must trust the future to the one who knows us by name and rise above our despair. What is our purpose? Paul said it: "For me, to live is Christ and to die is gain." Our purpose is to center in the risen Lord and look at every aspect of life from that lofty perch. Our purpose is to choose hope.

Christ knows about the trauma with our jobs, the pain in our marriages, the gaps between us and our children, and our frazzled nerves. Like the hairs of our heads, so our troubles are numbered. Knowing this, we must release them to his care and get on with our living.

What we're talking about here is a matter of perspective. God has never promised to meet all our expectations. It is foolhardy to assume that a relationship with the Lord will deliver a person from all trauma. Problems still develop. Tragedy continues to strike. Confusion rears its ugly head. Nevertheless, that person who chooses hope remains one notch above all this nonsense. The purpose smothers the pain.

Washington Irving picked up this truth when he observed, "Great minds have purposes; little minds have wishes. Little minds are subdued by misfortunes; great minds rise above them."

We started this examination by talking about the gap between what we are on the inside and what we do on the outside. I think it safe to observe that there will always be variances between human feelings and human performances. It is a matter of security. One has to be absolutely, dead-square, unequivocally secure, to practice the vulnerability of letting the inside . . . out.

A COMMON CONDITION

Several years ago a psychology professor administered a personality analysis to a class of graduate students. These people were blue-chippers, all targeting themselves for doctoral work. A few days later he passed out envelopes with the results, then stood back and watched as each of the students slipped deeper and deeper in their chairs. You see, he gave them all the same evaluation. It read like this:

1. You have a great need for other people to like and admire you.
2. You have a tendency to be critical of yourself.
3. You have a great deal of unused capacity which you have not turned to your advantage.
4. Your sexual adjustment has presented a problem for you.
5. Disciplined and self-controlled outside, you tend to be worrisome and insecure inside.
6. You pride yourself as an independent thinker and do not accept other's statements without satisfactory proof.
7. You have found it unwise to be frank in revealing yourself to others.
8. Security is one of your major goals in life.

They all bought it. They all accepted these deprecating descriptions of themselves. And so would you. And so would I. When they learned of his maneuver, they grasped the most valuable lesson he could teach them: Being human means being insecure.

A COMMON QUESTION

Do you know where you're going?
Are you a purposeful traveler?
Are your sights fixed on an appropriate horizon?
It was a blustery day in February 1967, when the professor of systematic theology walked to the front of the class with a little black book in his hand. The title? *Creative Brooding*. It had been composed by Robert Raines, a little-known preacher from Germantown, Pennsylvania, and it was about to make an unforgettable impression on one of the students—me.

"You guys [they were all guys at that time] are always looking for powerful preaching material. Well, this book is loaded," said the professor. "I want to share a summary of the challenge confronting every one of you."

With that, he began to read:

The joint, as Fats Waller would have said, was jumping. . . . And, during the last set, the saxophone player took off on a terrific solo. He was a kid from some insane place like Jersey City or Syracuse, but somewhere along the line he had discovered he could say it with a saxophone. He stood there, wide-legged, humping the air, filling his barrel chest, shivering in the rags of his twenty-odd years and screaming through the horn, "Do you love me?" "Do you love me?" "Do you love me?" And again—"Do you love me?" "Do you love me?" "Do you love me?" The same phrase unbearably, endlessly, and variously repeated with all the force the kid had. . . . The question was terrible and real. The boy was blowing with his lungs and guts out of his own short past; and somewhere in the past, in gutters or gang fights . . . in the acrid room, behind marijuana or the needles, under the smell in the precinct basement, he had received a blow from which he would never recover, and this no one wanted to believe. Do you love me? Do you love me? Do you love me? The men on the stand stayed with him cool and at a little distance, adding and questioning. . . . But each man knew that the boy was blowing for every one of them. (James Baldwin, *Another Country* [New York: Doubleday, 1960], pp. 13-14)

A lot of things have happened since those words were read in that classroom. The professor has retired and moved to Oregon. The author of the little book has served a stint as senior minister of the church I now lead. And the student, challenged then, is still challenged now, even as I write. Why? Because the question remains. It comes from every human being who ever tried to strike a balance between the inside and the outside. Do you love me?

I guess Bob Raines said it best at the end of that little episode. He wrote:

Do you love me?
You have let me suffer,
   and let me cause others to suffer.
You have watched me get broken,
   and go sour.
You have pounded me for my sins,
   and made me hard.

Lord, I know you love me
   and all of us.
   Speak tenderly to us
   Comfort me.*

LIBERTY, SECURITY, AND RISK

I suppose it is our innate lack of confidence that makes security so important to us. Even though we have been told scores of times how faithful God is to us, we are ever aware of our unfaithfulness to God, and that makes us suspicious of the Almighty's

---

Creative Brooding (New York: Macmillan, 168), p. 49

ongoing concern and comfort. Thus, when we must reach inside for the courage to hope, we do so with some trepidation. After all, if God can't count on us, why should we be so arrogant as to count on God? We want God's love, but we know we don't deserve it. We want total freedom, but we know we can't manage it. And we want to boldly march into the future, but the risk seems overwhelming.

What is hope, when the bank account is dry and the mortgage is due?

What is hope, when all the medicine fails and the doctor says, "Six months at best."

What is hope, when the kid stares you straight in the face and screams, "I don't give a damn what you think, I'm going anyhow!"

A NATURAL PROCESS

Every Christmas the scene is repeated thousands of times, all over America. I saw it in the fragrances department of the Marshall Field's store in Chicago. The little girl couldn't have been more than three, dressed in a red snowsuit complete with white fur-lined hood and mittens. It made her walk like a "shmoo" out of "Lil' Abner."

As I waited for a clerk to check on a specific perfume, the little one waddled between me and the counter. Just seeing her made my ears feel happy. I watched carefully as she extended her journey some twenty to thirty feet. She would go two or three steps and turn around (she had no choice; one can't look over the shoulder while wearing a snow suit) to see if her mother was still there.

She was an adorable study in security, liberty, and risk. She wanted to explore that store but she didn't want to lose sight of Mama. She wanted to peek around some corners, look at the people and decorations, but it was a perilous adventure because it meant establishing distance from the most important influence in her life. Adventure called, safety answered; the child was caught on the human tightrope in the middle.

We've all been there. Funny thing is, we don't outgrow it. To the contrary, the human tightrope is always there for all of us; we live in the tension between security and liberty.

How does one cling to what is important and still discover new truths?

How do we protect our flanks while pressing into the future?

How do we conquer the fear of losing everything even as we make a lifestyle of choosing hope and embracing fresh experiences, new concepts, and untested ideas?

We find some answers to those questions in the parable of the talents, located in Matthew 25. To paraphrase, a wealthy landowner did some character research on his servants. Embarking on a vacation, he entrusted each of them with a bankroll to see how he would manage. One received five thousand dollars, another two thousand, and the last, one thousand.

The first servant called his broker, dumped the money with Cincinnati Microwave, and doubled it. The second bought a rusted out MG, restored it, and doubled his. But the third guy just couldn't get over the tenacity of the boss. He had seen him throw a fit over a few long distance telephone calls. He knew he was a tough taskmaster. He also subscribed to the weekly newsletter of Howard Ruff, and all indications were the economy was in a real tailspin. So taking no risks, he stashed his thousand in a mayonnaise jar buried in his mother-in-law's rose garden.

Upon the master's return, he called in the three servants to see how they had done. In response to the ingenuity of the first two, he made each division managers, tripling their salaries. But the last one, the one who received a thouand and returned a thousand, he fired, and he gave his thousand to the one who listened when E. F. Hutton talked.

And then comes one of the most difficult phrases in the Bible: "For to every one who has will more be given, and he will have abundance; but from him who has not, even what he has will be taken away."

There are timely messages here for would-be riskers.

GIFTS AND TENSION

The flipside of every gift is tension. The more gifted we are, the more responsible we must be. The more secure we are on one hand, the more liberated we are on the other. It's the space in the middle that haunts us. Between security and liberation is the rocky road called "risk." It's where the toddler keeps looking back. It's where the tension builds.

Contrary to popular opinion, there is nothing wrong with tension. To be sure, without it, we cannot grow.

I think of the days of my youth when I would come home from school, grab my kite, and head for the cinder lot adjacent to the MaGirl Foundry in Bloomington, Illinois. The first twelve years of my life were spent in a typical middle-class residential area covered with World War II–vintage bungalows. They were placed elbow to elbow, with no room to fly a kite. Come spring, paper carcasses dotted the trees and telephone wires, to prove the point.

But the lot at MaGirl's was perfect. Half a city block long, it served as a parking area for day workers. But, at 3:30 in the afternoon, they went home and that parking lot became free space for any cautious kite flyer. I can remember, as if it were yesterday, doing "four rollers" on that lot. I'd let out four rolls of string. My kite would be out of sight. And it all started with about ten feet of slack and a quick sprint down the middle of that parking lot. The combination of space to run and the tension created by wind against the kite launched it without fail!

When God gives us gifts, we are also given space to run. Then, it becomes a matter of whether or not we are willing to live with tension.

The first two servants had no problem with that. They accepted the tension and lived with the risk. The third couldn't handle the pressure and subsequently forfeited his privilege.

With gifts come tension. We either use what God gives or lose what God gives. It's that simple.

This is not to endorse high blood pressure, drumming fingers, or overactive thyroid conditions. It is to explain that there is nothing wrong with tension when recognized as the natural terrain between security and liberty.

So how do we live with it?

We start by accepting God's role in it. Then we make it a point to properly position ourselves.

INTENTIONAL RISK

A few months ago, I gave the invocation at a banquet where the venerated Wayne Woodrow Hayes, longtime coach of the Ohio State Buckeyes, was the speaker. Halfway through his address, Woody took off on the evils of the forward pass. He explained the horror of "trajectory." That's what happens to the ball between the passer and the receiver. If it's perfect, the consequence is a completion. If not, two of the three possible effects of throwing a pass result: an incompletion or, perish the thought, an interception.

Woody then proceeded to explain why some defensive backs get more interceptions than others. It's a matter of courage and position. As soon as the quarterback drops back to pass, the tension is on. The defensive back has two choices. He can play it safe and simply stay far behind the receiver so as to make the tackle after the catch. Or, he can do the job right and position himself so as to appropriately step between the receiver and the ball at precisely the right moment.

The first choice minimizes risk.

The second maximizes opportunity.

Which one the player chooses depends on the degree of his security. In my opinion, this is also the difference between All-Americans and also-rans. The All-American believes in himself, and not fearing failure in pursuit of excellence, he'll opt for courage and position every time.

The same principle applies to using the gifts God has given us. We can bury them and stay the same, or risk and grow.

As I encounter fellow believers all over America, I sense the presence of hundreds of people who know what it is to risk. They've done it and they are doing it . . . right now!

Even as I write, I can hear those mental computers running out there, and the questions emerge: Is it not possible to be secure and liberated at the same time? Can we not concurrently hang on to what we have and exercise our freedom? Is it beyond reason to be tightfisted and on the grow? Can't we reach a point where we have amassed enough security so that no risk intimidates us?

The Bible gives us some answers. It tells us it

depends on where our security is located. If our security is in our titles, businesses, bankrolls, or estates, the answer is *no!* In fact, if our security is anywhere other than in the echo of that empty tomb, we are standing on sand. Our security and our hope issue from the same source, the resurrected Lord.

TRUE SECURITY

I believe this is why the Master explained that it was easier for a camel to pass through the eye of a needle than for a rich man to enter the kingdom of God. Clinging to temporal security, we cannot claim eternal security. To grab the second, one must release the first.

So let us return to Marshall Field's. That toddler was filled with anxiety because she had not come to terms with her mother's love. She thought she could get lost on her own. She did not take into account the fact that her mother wasn't about to let her go too far. Her security was not in what she was doing but what her mother was letting her do.

And the words of the psalmist leap into my consciousness:

I lift up my eyes to the hills.
  From whence does my help come?
My help comes from the Lord,
  who made heaven and earth.
. . . .
The Lord will keep
  your going out and your coming in
  from this time forth and forevermore.

(Psalm 121:1, 2, 8)

If we think we can ever be secure in our own actions, we are dreadfully mistaken. But if we think we can be anything but secure when we trust in God, we are even more mistaken.

To hope in the Lord is to willingly run against the wind. Risk in the arms of the Lord is not risk, it is simply adventure.

The modern proverb hits the mark: "The dice of God are always loaded."

In light of this truth, the most grievous of all sins is to "sit on our hands," satisfied with life the way it is—to bask in the bounty of the day.

God has been good to us. We live in the finest country on earth. That is a gift. We enjoy health and prosperity unknown to any previous generation of human beings. That is a gift. Our educational system has honed our minds to the point where we can read, write, and rationalize with the best of them. That is a gift.

But the flipside of every gift is tension, and the answer to tension is attitude, and the key to attitude is security, not in ourselves, but in him.

KEEP MOVING

Recall with me the wonderful experience on Mount Tabor. Early in his ministry, Jesus took Peter and James and John and went up on the mountain to pray. Even as the Master prayed, we read that he was transformed, his garment dazzled white, and Moses and Elijah joined him. This was God's affirmation, not only of what Jesus had done, but what he would do.

Seeing all this, Peter played the predictable role. "Quick," he exclaimed, "let's build a shrine on this spot!" He wanted to freeze the moment, to preserve forever the fabulous feeling that filled his heart. But Christ would have none of that. He led them down off the mountain and sent them out to serve!

With each day, God affirms believers with the promise of eternity. The resurrection stands as a bold pronouncement that every person is unique, unrepeatable, and loved forever. Still, I think we err greatly if we decide to build a shrine every time we sense God's blessing. Let us not drop the mainsail and dock the ship. And let us not break stride for the sake of celebration.

It is always a temptation to make of great moments ends in themselves. Let that temptation pass. What we are given today is but a foretaste of what will be required tomorrow.

THE NEED FOR FLEXIBILITY

If we are to choose hope and lay claim to the future, we must be courageous enough to risk what we have and open enough to accept what God gives. Openness is the final dimension of a paradigm of hope.

Perhaps it is my sheltered background, but I find gambling casinos to have a sinister silence about them. I first noticed it several years ago on Paradise Island in Nassau. It was my first visit to a gambling hall, and I distinctly recall the plush carpet, the ripple of card against card, an occasional jingle from a generous slot machine, and the subdued mumble of the blackjack players. Normally, in a room filled with five hundred people, one would never hear such gentle audio effects. But in a casino, people walk differently, talk differently, and breathe differently.

I also distinctly remember, with occasional assistance, that on that visit my wife Celeste won and I lost. I'm a lousy gambler. Ever confident that my ship will come in, I most often paddle home in a figurative rubber raft.

Nevertheless on our last visit to the Carribean,

while waiting for a floor show in San Juan, I ventured into another casino, not to play, but to watch. I noticed, immediately, an exorbitant number of people clustered around one of the tables. Hence, like a gawker near a freeway accident, I slowed my pace and headed for the action. After weaseling between a few folks, I spotted the main attraction. A middle-aged gentleman with graying temples and a whisper voice was on a streak at a blackjack table. Seven or eight stacks of blue chips were in front of him. Hand after hand, he would just push a stack forward and nod to the dealer. Every time, the crowd would react. No gasps, mind you, these people are cool. It was a matter of folded arms, wry glances, and facial twitches. But like everything else in a casino, every gesture seemed magnified.

I didn't understand what was so important until a woman beside me, looking down, whispered, "Five hundred dollars a chip!"

Now, I nearly knocked a man over pressing forward to count the chips. There were twenty in each stack. Ten thousand dollars a hand—a smidgen out of my league.

The call for the floor show forced me to leave. I don't know how "Stack-Man" fared, but I do know this, for the first forty minutes of the floor show, I didn't see much. All I could think about was the velvet abandon with which the man played that game.

I thought of him again as I outlined this chapter. The second verse of the twelfth chapter of Paul's letter to the Christians in Rome has always been a favorite of mine, but in the context of hope, it has even more significance. "Do not be conformed to this world, but be transformed by the renewal of your mind, that you may prove what is the will of God, what is good and acceptable and perfect."

For me, hope is the essence of being *transformed by the renewal of your mind*. When we hope, we assume a distinct advantage on worry, anxiety, and despair. We are free to enjoy the world and to escape the world at the same time. "Stack-Man" was not conformed to this world. Sure, he was toying at a temporal pursuit. But, he was above it, almost disdainful, free to win because he was free to lose. He was more secure than the circumstance in which he was living.

Most of us would have been basket cases, palms sweaty, nerves on end, six breaths from a coronary. Why? Because we couldn't afford it? Oh, perhaps a few could. But, I don't think that's the issue. I think the issue is a matter of attitude. It's a matter of the renewal of one's mind.

A CHANGE OF MIND

I believe hope renews the mind.

I have a good friend who spent eighteen months in Vietnam. He doesn't talk about it often, but when he does, he always talks about attitude. He says that when he first went over he was "faithfully fatalistic" about the whole thing. "If God wants me to die in Vietnam, I'll die in Vietnam. If not, I won't. Why worry?"

That worked just fine until he had but thirty days left. Suddenly, his attitude changed. Now it was up to him. He says he wore his flak jacket everywhere. He worked in it. He played in it. He slept in it. Survival became an obsession with him. He couldn't eat. He couldn't sleep. He couldn't think. And he was miserable company.

Then one night, his location came under a heavy mortar attack. One of the shells landed so close the impact flipped him out of his bunk, with the latter coming to rest on top of him. He says that was the moment when his mind was transformed again. Lying there under his sleeping bag, he started to laugh. It came to him that nothing had changed since the day he arrived in Vietnam. God was still in charge and the divine plan for his life was still in effect. It was necessary to be wise, to take precautions and attempt to survive. It was not necessary to make himself miserable in an effort to manipulate the margins of life. His hope was not in his ability to handle the situation but in God's plan for his life.

He had been "transformed by the renewal of his mind."

If choosing hope has any effect on our lives, it should be to make of all of us faithful fatalists. We do our best and leave God the rest.

Here we run into an interesting bonus. When we trust the Master, we find the Master.

A SUDDEN CLARITY

Having surrendered our lives to the care and keeping of Jesus Christ, we are soon amazed at how much easier it is to see him at work in our midst.

Remember the old black and white gangster movies, where the safecracker would sit in front of the safe and sand his fingertips? That wasn't a matter of Mafia masochism, it was a means of sensitizing touch so as to feel the trip points in the lock. It was preparation to feel what could not be predicted.

Choosing hope challenges us to open our minds to the possibilities that God comes to us in unexpected ways, at unexpected moments, in unexpected places. Who would have predicted the birth of God's Son between a goat and a cow? And why do we insist that what happened then, God's speaking in unexpected ways, cannot happen now?

The secret, it seems to me, is to make a lifestyle of being ready to receive him.

Annie Dillard points to the locked corridors of the average human mind when she talks about a man who is teaching a stone to talk. The subtlety of her message underlines the point I am trying to make.

The island where I live is peopled with cranks like myself. In a cedar-shake shack on a cliff is a man in his thirties who lives alone with a stone he is trying to teach to talk.

Wisecracks on this topic abound, as you might expect, but they are made as it were perfunctorily, and mostly by the young. For in fact, almost everyone here respects what Larry is doing, as I do. . . .

It could be, for instance, a pinch of sand he is teaching to talk, or a prolonged northerly, or any one of a number of waves. But it is, in fact, I assure you, a stone. It is—for I have seen it—a palm-sized oval beach cobble whose dark grey is cut by a band of white which runs around and, presumably, through it; such stones we call "wishing stones," for reasons obscure but not, I think, unimaginable.

He keeps it on a shelf. Usually the stone lies protected by a square of untanned leather, like a canary asleep under its cloth. Larry removes the cover for the stone's lessons, or more accurately, I should say, for the ritual or rituals which they perform together several times a day.

No one knows what goes on at these sessions, least of all myself, for I know Larry but slightly, and that owing only to a mix-up in our mail. I assume that like any other meaningful effort, the ritual involves sacrifice, the suppression of self-consciousness; and a certain precise tilt of the will, so that the will becomes transparent and hollow, a channel for the work. I wish him well. It is a noble work, and beats, from any angle, selling shoes. (*Teaching a Stone to Talk* [New York: Harper & Row, 1982], p. 68)

So we sit here in our flak jackets convinced that the fate of civilization is in our hands, knowing that stones can't talk and cancer can't be cured and some idiot is bound to push the button. We find our vision shrinking and our nerves coming apart because we know full well we can't manage the world around us.

What we really need is a jolt that will flip us under our bunks and remind us who is in charge.

THE PROMISE OF HOPE

If we could only trust, if we could only believe, if we could only be transformed by the renewal of our minds, we could discover that within the working of the Spirit of God stones can talk, cancer can be cured, nerves can be restored, jobs can be found, children can come home, and

The wolf shall dwell with the lamb,
and the leopard shall lie down with the kid,
and the calf and the lion and the fatling together,
and a little child shall lead them.

(Isaiah 11:6)

Have you ever noticed how people who think they are lucky *are* lucky? Know why? I believe it is because they are constantly preparing themselves for great experiences. Open to fortune, they find it. It may not come exactly as anticipated. To be sure, it rarely does. Still, because they are willing to positively adjust, they perpetually receive. Sometimes they don't know it until long after the point of blessing, but nonetheless, God affirms them time and again.

Choosing hope means being open to fortune.

I see a father and a son sprawled on a dusty hayrack on a farm in the heart of Iowa. It's dusk and they are watching the sun settle over a field they plowed together just hours earlier. Like statues (big and little),

93

their poses are similar: tummy down, elbows out, chin on hand.

The boy speaks. "Dad?"

"Yeah."

"See that curve in the furrows, starting way up on top of the hill and working its way clear down to the fence?"

"Uh-huh."

"What caused it?"

"A rock up at the top. Didn't see it, bounced the plow three feet to the right."

"And you followed the pattern?"

"Right."

"It's beautiful."

"I know."

Sometimes we must reach the twilight of the day before we look back and see the touch of the Master in its midst. Years can pass before we note the wonderful will of God in the bump of a rock that changed our course.

So my thoughts return to "Stack-Man" in the casino. In a relative sense, what he was doing doesn't compare with what most of us do every day. He was shoving chips around, maneuvering barter. We deal with an even more precious commodity—life itself.

If he had the confidence allowing him to be cool under pressure, how much more do those who have been transformed by the renewal of their minds command? How much more dwells in the hands of the children of hope?

We have what Annie Dillard described as a "tilt of the will," the capacity to receive God's love when others can't even see it. For us, stones can talk, cancer can be cured, life can turn around, the lion can lie down with the lamb, peace can be achieved, and life can last forever.

4

Maintaining Hope

SHAKING AND MOVING

As we attempt to keep hope in the center of our lives, there are two influences essential to our success. First, we must maintain a sense of momentum. Hope is not conducive to stationary deployment. It calls for a sense of vitality, an ongoing feeling that what we are involved with in the present is important to the future. The worst thing a believer can do is commit to a positive future, then sit down and relax. The challenge is to keep growing toward the future. Second, we must be prepared for change. I believe it was Cardinal Newman who said, "To grow is to change and to have changed often is to have grown much."

These two dimensions are inextricably bound together; momentum feeds on change and change is enabled by momentum. If it's been a while since we have stretched our faith, we'll have to be very intentional about growth. Nonetheless, it is virtually impossible to choose hope without simultaneously embracing change and momentum. Christ knew this and placed the challenge clearly before his disciples.

DROPPING THE GAUNTLET

It was a gathering of eagles, free spirits, people on the grow. He was talking to the renegades, the searchers, the misfits who were willing to go against the grain. "Jesus then said to the Jews who had believed in him, 'If you continue in my word, you are truly my disciples, and you will know the truth, and the truth will make you free' " (John 8:31-32).

He was talking to "the Jews who had believed in him."

What courageous people they must have been. Maintaining a Christian lifestyle in our world is nothing compared to what these people were up against. At the worst, we may be the victims of condescending smiles and occasional social ostracism, but these poor folks were total outcasts. Judaism is a national religion. Hence, those who left the fold forfeited class, status, and birthright. Whatever chance of success, comfort, and security might have existed for a Jew under the heel of Augustus Caesar was reduced 90 percent when that same Jew gave allegiance to the Nazarene carpenter.

Nobody knew this better than Jesus himself. Thus, sensing the tough road which was in front of them, the Lord shared a single phrase which sets the tone for all who would be children of hope: "if you continue in my word."

More than any other words of the Master, I believe those words underscore the power of momentum in the Christian faith.

THE STILL–FRAME MINDSET

Recall with me the spectacular advertising campaign of the Canon AE-1. For several years it has been one of the hottest-selling cameras on the market. Much of this success is due to characters like Joe Theisman, Ben Crenshaw, and Stan Smith. Wanting to underline the speed of the camera, the advertisers selected these action-oriented sports figures to promote it, as it caught them in stop-action doing their thing—Theisman throwing a football, Crenshaw stroking a putt, Smith smashing a serve.

It was good advertising. It made us watch the commercial just to see the freeze-frame on the star. In the meantime, it bathed our brains with positive vibrations about the AE-1. It also provides a brilliant illustration of the human tendency to park at the peaks. Unfortunately, we see most of life's key events as locked in space and time, just like those freeze-frame shots of the stars.

When we talk about education, we record degrees and the dates on which they were given. When we talk about love, we lean toward major events and datable experiences, particularly anniversaries. And when we talk about faith, we often freeze-frame the process by pointing to so-called spiritual birthdays, years of membership in the church, and a list of tasks we have completed in the name of the Lord.

Like still cameras, our minds convert animated events that would naturally lead to further development into static points supposedly sufficient unto themselves. Consequently, one of the most popular phrases in any church is—and the older the church, the more popular the phrase—"I've paid my dues, let somebody else do it!"

But Christ said, "If you continue in my word, you will know the truth, and the truth will make you free."

When I arrived at First Community Church, I was not very impressed with the building. As the months passed, I became increasingly fond of the style of the old edifice. It has a special character, a warmth rarely found in contemporary architecture. Still, I'd like to pick a bone with the person who placed the inscription over the front door. It only tells half the story. It underlines the consequence but avoids the game plan. It says only, "You shall know the truth and the truth shall make you free." For me, the prefix "If you continue in my word" needs to be added.

In the Greek, "If you continue in my word" is, "Ean meinete en to loyo." The key word is *meinete*, the root of which is *menw*, which means "to abide or dwell." Hence, what the Master really said was, "If you abide in my word, you will know the truth and the truth will make you free." That is not a static process. It is not a datable experience. It is an ongoing development. It does not end. Those "continuing in the word" are forever under construction.

THE HARD–HAT SYNDROME

Several months ago, I made a call in the Huntington National Bank building in downtown Columbus. When I left the building I attempted to cut through a construction zone next door. I wasn't twenty yards into the area before a security officer stopped me. "I'm sorry, sir, you can't go through here. This is a hard-hat area," he explained. I meekly excused myself and proceeded to walk around the block. Then, I sat in my car for a moment and watched that "hard-hat area." A crane was hoisting concrete to an upper floor. Workmen were tossing plywood four floors to the ground. A truck load of marble slabs was delivered. All within a ten-minute period. It was a hive of activity. I could see why it was a "hard-hat area." Anybody strolling around in there had to be ready for action!

When Christ instructed us to abide in *his* Word, he

was sending all of us into a "hard-hat area" as well. The Word of God is not static. It is not a neat little book we can investigate whenever we feel like it. It is a life-force that covers every moment of our lives. The Word of God is any medium expressing God's love and guidance for all humanity. To "abide in the word" is to be ever sensitive to what *God* is doing with you, through you, and in you.

Education is not a do-it-and-get-it-done-with process. Wise persons know it never stops; they "abide" in a world of developing information and extended experiences. Love is not a do-it-and-get-it-done-with process. Successful relationships depend on constant cultivation and renewal; they "abide" in a world of caring, sharing, touching, and listening. And hope is not a do-it-and-get-it-done-with process. It demands a practiced sensitivity to every moment as a gift from God and a hotbed for holy communication.

This underlines a persistent problem for contemporary Christians. Our lives are so cluttered with conflicting demands that we are lucky to find one hour of every week in which to worship. Thus, if we are to continue in his Word, we must develop new awareness that when we do not come to Christ, he has a marvelous way of coming to us.

THE KEY EVENT

The resurrection is not only a significant event for those who choose hope solely because it marks a victory over death. It is also significant because it illustrates God's capacity to work outside the limits of human experience. Life in light of that resurrection is life aware that God can communicate when nobody else can, if we are sensitive to the Word in our midst. Hope feeds on that truth.

During my ministry, many have shared with me their skepticism about the resurrection. That's OK, but never to the point where the limitations of personal perception block the possibilities of God's action. Our minds must never blind us to what God is doing in our lives. Like Thomas in the Upper Room, we are free to express our doubt but challenged to remain open to further developments.

If the first part of "abiding in the Word" is a matter of remaining open to God's action, the second might logically be the active pursuit of the Master's will in our lives.

The tragedy of freeze-frame Christianity is the way it robs us of new riches in faith.

So you have been a Christian for forty years, so you have been a church member for twenty-seven, the question remains: Are you growing in Christ or sitting still? Are your spiritual horizons expanding or contracting?

A CALL FOR RESEARCH AND DEVELOPMENT

Four years ago, America experienced a stunning loss. For the first time in over one hundred years—in fact, the first time ever—the America's Cup was not on American soil. It was "down under." The Aussies wrested it from us in a dramatic series of yacht races off the coast of Newport, Rhode Island.

The late Red Smith once referred to the America's Cup races as "the most absurdly overplayed event in sports." He insinuated that the whole thing was a joke, a fix in charge of the New York Yacht Club, which sets the rules to assure American victories year after year.

Not in 1983. Australia II was so superior that not even rule manipulations could save the cup. Truth was, it was about time. Nevertheless, it would never have happened apart from the exalted research of Ben Lexcen. While America's millionaires assumed yacht development had reached an impasse, Lexcen refused to believe it, went one step further, changed the keel of the Australian craft, and snatched the cup.

The moral of the story? Learning never ceases. There is always more to come. To abandon the search is to forego the discovery. That truth is as fitting for the Christian faith as for the world of yachting, cancer research, energy development, or any other field of

We are finite human beings, forever under construction. When believers accept that truth, their horizons explode!

I think of the mountain climber who stands on the plain and targets a majestic peak. Then, as the adventure unfolds, he discovers every summit reached reveals another yet to come. So it is with the Christian faith. The quest is never ended. We are forever searchers. The Greek root for the word "disciple" is *mathetes*; literally translated, it means "learner."

Are you a learner? Is your faith a continuing expedition into the will of God in your life, or have you been the same kind of Christian for years? Do you feel the wind in your face, or are you locked in a fixed position, the same yesterday, today, and forever?

Ralph Waldo Emerson summarized the challenge. "God offers to every mind its choice between truth and repose. Take which you please . . . you can never have both!"

Many years ago, before it became popular to walk up the sides of skyscrapers in pursuit of publicity, a fellow named Philippe Petit was arrested after having walked a tightrope that he and his friends had shot between the twin towers of the New York World Trade Center. They took him directly to a psychiatric hospital. When they found him sane and in good spirits, they asked, "But why, why do you want to walk on a tightrope between the highest towers of the city and risk your life?" Petit, seemingly puzzled by the question, said, "Well, if I see three oranges, I have to juggle, and if I see two towers, I have to walk."

There is an inner drive that comes with abiding in the Word. It is a drive that makes the child of hope read a book, take a class, join a prayer group, and listen when others talk. It is a drive that keeps one perpetually in a spiritual "hard-hat area."

UNCHANGING CHANGE

At the conclusion of his most recent sojourn with Harry Angstrom, John Updike paints a stirring picture for all middle-aged men. We find "Rabbit" seated in the den as his wife and daughter-in-law jabber upstairs. Suddenly, the younger woman slips up beside the hero and places his granddaughter in his lap.

And Teresa comes softly down the one step into his den and deposits into his lap what he has been waiting for. Oblong cocooned little visitor, the baby shows her profile blindly in the shuddering flashes of color jerking from the Sony TV, the stitchless seam of the closed eyelid aslant, lips bubbled forward beneath the whorled nose as if in delicate disdain. She knows she's good. You can feel in the curve of the cranium she's feminine, that shows from the first day. Through all this she was pushed to be here, in his lap, his hands, a real presence hardly weighing anything but alive. Fortune's hostage, heart's desire, a granddaughter. Another nail in his coffin. (*Rabbit Is Rich* [New York: Alfred A. Knopf, 1981], p. 467)

The whole Rabbit trilogy is Updike's analysis of the flow of life. But somehow, the thought of the cavalier high school basketball star, now a grandfather, cradling a child and owning his mortality is terribly disturbing. Particularly for those in the second half of life.

Why can we not choose a point in the trip and fix ourselves in it?

Why can we not freeze the march of time and bask forever in the fullness of health and the splendor of youth?

Why do eyes dim and joints stiffen?

Why does energy wane and memory lapse?

Why do computers replace people and new theories displace old truths?

What ever happened to FDR, Arthur Godfrey, and Boston Blackie?

Some sage once quipped, "The only thing that never changes is change itself." So if change is life's only constant, how does it influence our effort to maintain hope in an age of skepticism?

THE MARCH OF TIME

Change never changes. It is always there even though we do everything in our power to reinforce the status quo. I suppose this was never more obvious to me than a year or so ago when one of the television networks ran a special on Cape Kennedy. I've always had a warm spot for the space program, probably because that probing, risky adventure paralleled a similar period in my life. When John Glenn first orbited the earth, I was a naïve, buzz-headed college student trying to adjust to life away from home. I watched his valor, along with a score of other

Wheaton College hopefuls, on a television monitor in a campus dining hall.

Later, having graduated from seminary and settled in my first church, I took a group of high school students to Florida to watch the launch that put Neil Armstrong on the moon. I can still see the huge rocket, the superstructure around it, and the thousands of people parked bumper to bumper along adjacent highways to watch history in the making.

Hence, you can imagine my surprise when the cameras revealed some of those same launching pads now overgrown with weeds. The superstructures are decaying with rust, and many local motels, once booked for months in advance, stand boarded and abandoned, victims of skipping American fancy and the march of time.

I understand that some of the old glitter has returned with the Space Shuttle program, and I hope the recent disaster doesn't dampen the spirit, but still it was quite a shock to see what was in 1969 the cutting edge of civilization infested with weeds less than twenty years later.

What was Harvey Cox's line? "Not to decide is to decide and not to journey is to journey anyway." Well, we can add another: "Not to change is to change in spite of yourself."

Where we get in trouble is when we try to hang on to yesterday as a substitute for tomorrow.

CLINGING TO A MYTH

I am reminded of the melon traps employed by the Zulus to capture the wily ring-tailed monkey. These little creatures are fast and tricky. The hunters love them as they are the most popular export for zoos all over the world, adapting well to other climates.

Legend has it that a small boy devised today's ingenious means of catching the monkeys, after having accidentally witnessed a ferocious fight between two ring-tails over a broken melon. It appeared as if they were willing to die for the delicate seeds. Afterward, the boy cut a small hole, just big enough for a monkey's hand, in the side of a melon and sat it in a clearing. Within moments, a ring-tail spotted the melon and jumped down to investigate. Finding the hole, it stuck its hand in, grabbing a handful of seeds. Now it had a problem—either drop the seeds, or leave its hand in the melon. The hole was not sufficient to allow the hand, now bulging with seeds, to pass through.

At this point, the lad stepped forward and tossed a net over the monkey. Even then, the monkey would not release the seeds.

Today, such melon traps are a common site near Zulu villages.

By clinging to the past, we do not avoid change, we simply strip it of its significance. We get trapped, like ring-tailed monkeys. Our challenge is to view change as opportunity rather than an assault on what is meaningful to us. The Gemini program was spectacular; the Skylab project was even better. One builds on the other.

Russell Baker, the syndicated columnist, addressed this in a column about the old phrase, "You can't get there from here." He explains that the "there" is the past. We can recall it, we can be influenced by it, and we can learn from it, but we cannot return to it. We live in the "here," and the prudent person makes a lifestyle of combining "here" and "there" to go "somewhere" in the future.

Do you realize every seven years 90 percent of the cells in your body are new? Change takes place without our permission. It is essential to life.

I believe this is the point to which our Lord was

referring when he told the plastic-coated Pharisees, "The kingdom of God is not coming with signs to be observed; nor will they say, 'Lo, here it is!' or 'There!' for behold, the kingdom of God is in the midst of you" (Luke 17:20-21).

ALL AROUND US

Truth is, the most significant changes are generally effected from the inside out. They happen slowly, over a period of time, and rarely in the manner in which we anticipate them.

Again, the writing of Robert Grudin makes the point.

In late November of 1968, I spent a few days in a hotel just off the Piazza San Marco in Venice. At six one morning, hearing the loud warning bells, I jumped out of bed, grabbed my camera and rushed out to see the famous Venetian flood. I stood in the empty and as yet dry Piazza and looked out toward the Gulf, for I expected the flood tides to come in from the open water. Many minutes passed before I turned to see that the Piazza was flooding, not directly from the Gulf, but up through its own sewers. The indented gratings in the pavement had all but disappeared under calm, flat silver puddles, which grew slowly and silently until their peripheries touched and the Piazza had become a lake. That morning I experienced vividly, if almost subliminally, the reality of change itself, how it fools our sentinels and undermines our defenses, how careful we are to look for it in the wrong places, how it does not reveal itself until it is beyond redress, how vainly we search for it around us and find too late that it has occurred within us. (*Time and the Art of Living*, p. 9)

"Behold, the kingdom of God is in the midst of you!" That's how it happens. We make ourselves available to Christ. We open to him. We commit to walk in his way, and suddenly, the expected gives way to the unexpected, the predictable becomes unpredictable, and the cobwebs and dust of life under the dominance of self are swept away by the dynamics of the Holy Spirit working in us sixty minutes every hour, twenty-four hours every day, seven days every week.

Shortly after my arrival at First Community Church, one of my new friends came in to see me. We talked about a lot of things, and then he started talking to me about his commitment to the church. He said, "I'm already tithing and I want to increase my assistance for the Operating Funds Campaign, but it's this media project that has me worried. I want to help but can't see how."

I restrained myself from hugging him on the spot. (Tithers are not that easy to find in old mainline churches.) Then, I shared my belief about faith commitments. You see, when we trust the future to God, blessings come from unexpected places. The essence of a faith commitment is not an analysis of our financial capacity; it is not a matter of balancing the checkbook; it is not a question of supporting particular programs. The essence of a faith commitment is a matter of will. Do we want to support God's work or not? If we do, we can.

I remember the counsel of a veteran preacher who once said to me, "Barry, trust God to make good changes in your life. Get on your knees and pray, 'Lord, if you will provide, I will give!' Then, stand back, son, he will provide!"

I shared that story with my friend, and I could see the relief in his eyes. When his pledge card came in it included the handwritten words, "If the Lord pro-

vides, I will give." A year later he told me he was going
to do the same thing again. No sweat.

Do you understand that principle? Christ doesn't
want your money. He wants your will. Once you place
him first in your life, you'll never again squirm during
a church operating funds campaign.

ASSUMING A NEW PARTNER

Now, it is extremely important that we understand
the cumulative influence of releasing the will and
trusting change to the ultimate purpose of God. The
more faithfully we trust the Lord, the more diligently
he works in our lives.

There is an energy discovered when one accepts the
lordship of Christ. It is greater than any power
humans can achieve. It exceeds the parameters of
politics. It surpasses the influence of wealth. And it
dwarfs the shallow consequences of fame and
recognition. It is an inner peace conceived in the
knowledge that Jesus Christ is forever at your side.

Dick Stegner played a major role in my life by
teaching me to unlock the Greek language. He was the
youngest of all my seminary mentors. Raised in
Cincinnati, he was heavily influenced by the Roman
Catholic Church, although at the time I met him he
was a full-fledged Methodist.

One afternoon he was musing about his Ohio
childhood when he said, "I think I'll always be a little
Catholic just for the statue." This brought guffaws
from the students, who thought he was referring to
dashboard icons. He was not.

Raising his hand to calm the hilarity, he told of an
incident with one of his parents that made us all think
deeply about our commitments to Jesus Christ. It's
been a long time since I heard the story, but I think it

involved his mother. At any rate, young Dick was struggling with the whole question of Christanity, or maybe "rebelling" would be a better word. He didn't want to go to church. He didn't want to read the Bible. He didn't want to pray. He didn't want to do anything that had to do with God. Desperate to convey his feelings to his mother, he stated flatly and firmly, "Faith is nothing, Mother. It is nothing!"

With that, she snatched him by the hand and they headed for the church. He resisted, she persisted, and after a long struggle they finally arrived at the front of the church. "I'm not going in, Mom!" he said.

"Don't have to," came the response, "just look at this." And she pointed at the feet of a statue of the Holy Mother. One foot was placed in front of the other in much the same style employed by fashion models when standing still. But the forward foot was half missing. It wasn't chipped off, or cut off. It was just gently rounded.

As the boy's mind raced for an explanation, his mother made her point. "So faith is nothing, huh, Richard? Well, tell that to the thousands of believers who have kissed that foot every time they visited the church."

Stone conquered by kisses, worn away by millions of whisper touches. The only people who would find that silly are those who have never known devotion beyond the self.

I feel sorry for people who can't commit themselves without perfect proof. And I feel challenged by those who have mastered the art of simple trust.

Change never changes. Neither does God. Choosing hope means to trust the latter and to welcome the former.

5

Hope and the Oppressed

So I sit here in my plush suburban home and write about hope. Easy for me to do. Of course I have hope. Why wouldn't I? I have power. I have privilege. I have mobility. I have a bank account. I have a steady job and a blossoming career. Hope? No problem.

But what about the guy who just lost his job? Or the street person? Or the mother who can't afford anything better than dog food for her baby? What about the black person who can't afford an education and can't get a job without one? What about the person of a divergent lifestyle dubbed sick by society, satanic by some in the church?

If our hope is based on the love of Christ for all humanity, then we had best pay attention to the oppressed. If they have no hope, how authentic is ours?

THE CRY OF THE OPPRESSED

For two decades, the oppressed have been a dominant force on the American value system. First, it was the civil rights movement; next, the emergence of women's liberation; and now, the awakening of homosexuals to the right to dignity. With the exception of women, each of these groups represents a relatively small portion of the general populace. Nevertheless, they have managed to shape political, educational, economic, and religious policy with alarming consistency. The secret? One undeniable claim common to minority and majority alike: "I've got a right to be me!"

We need to understand that liberation wouldn't be necessary if oppression did not exist. If freedom is the goal, bondage must be the reality. Thus, in imparting hope to the oppressed our first challenge is to help them shatter their bonds.

When we are oppressed, how do we respond? For most of us, the answer is quick and easy. We fight back. Negative force generates negative force. You shout at me, I shout at you. You muscle me, I muscle you. You hold me down, and sooner or later, I will bite your hand.

Let us learn by the example and effectiveness of the gentle Nazarene. Oppressed by hate, he responded with grace. He didn't fight and he didn't give up the cause either. He simply changed the pattern. He met violence with quiet confidence. He responded to power with peace. And he overcame malice with a gentle touch and a genuinely caring attitude.

Militancy, then, for any purpose, must be seen as a negative, destructive force. At best, it sounds an alarm more easily and effectively communicated otherwise. At worst, it forces people to choose sides purely as a means of defense.

So how did Christ respond to oppression? Consider these words: "Judge not, that you be not judged. For with the judgment you pronounce you will be judged, and the measure you give will be the measure you get.

Why do you see the speck that is in your brother's eye, but do not notice the log that is in your own eye?" (Matthew 7:1-3).

Oppression is the unjust exercise of power, the practice of devaluing other human beings, the habit of passing judgment on others by the manner in which we control and direct their freedom. It is a blatant negation of hope.

THE CALL TO LIBERATION

Ultimately, liberation is a personal issue. It does not belong to the masses. It is misplaced when tied to a group. Gay rights, black rights, and women's rights are only as strong as the individuals involved. The hope that must be shared with all oppressed people is that any one of them, no matter where he or she happens to be, will be accorded the basic right to dignity, freedom, and opportunity.

Recently, at a special leadership seminar, Kempton Hewitt, dean of Methesco Seminary, described the issues he thinks will be challenging the church at the turn of the century. Among them he included a renewal of conflict in America over civil rights. His position? Since the sixties we have learned to talk an inclusive language, but we have yet to embrace an inclusive socioeconomic system.

For some, even the language hasn't changed. And even for those of us who have made it a point to avoid racist, sexist language, we still manage to condone it through acquiescent silence. People still speak of wops, spics, niggers, polacks, and wetbacks. They talk of fruits, faggots, dykes, and homos. Meanwhile, we stand silent and with every word the barrier between the children of hope and the children of despair grows stronger.

So long as we can keep people lumped into groups, or pass judgments through some para-personal formula (biblical or otherwise), we don't have to deal with the fact that neither Christ's cross nor his empty tomb were asterisk equipped. Both remain unconditional. For me, nothing seems more inconsistent with the person of Jesus Christ than a proof-texted assault on the dignity of another human being. My guess is, had the Master been present at the recent demonstrations in San Francisco, he would have been affirming the demonstrators while demeaning their tactics.

Columnist Sidney Harris isolates the issue: "Stupid people define others by where they come from; intelligent people, by where they are going; wise people, by how they conduct themselves from point to point, no matter what their origin or destination" (*Pieces of Eight* [Boston: Houghton Mifflin, 1981], p. 29).

When minds fall victim to stereotypes, minds need remodeling. The value of a person is not a matter of birth, skin pigment, sex, or sexual preference. It's a matter of the soul. Everybody's got one, and Christ died for every one.

Paul undoubtedly displayed cultural blindness in some of these areas, but in spite of the Apostle's writing I can't imagine our Lord turning his back on any person in response to a variant lifestyle. As the biblical record indicates, the Master got upset with folks only when they started hurting others, only when they practiced oppression.

THE COST OF BEING DIFFERENT

At the same time as we affirm the right to divergent lifestyles, both majority and minority must accept the fact that being different takes a toll. Whether it is fair or not, the majority nearly always has an advantage.

For example, we live in a right-handed world. A quick visit to a sporting goods store makes this abundantly clear, as right-handed gear outnumbers left-handed gear six to one. It only stands to reason. The market leans to the right. Hence, there is a measure of oppression for left-handers. They pay a price for their minority status.

This is a dilemma common to all minorities. It is not a matter of personal value or selective judgment. It is not a matter of being wrong. Truth is, there is nothing wrong with being different. But by the standards of Jesus Christ, there is a lot wrong with rejecting the different for no other reason than their differences. The essence of bigotry is the categorical condemnation of variant lifestyles.

FEAR OF MEGABLUR

Here, I want to explain a lingering personal fear. It is the fear that as differences are minimized—and I pray they will be—we will be lost in our sameness; humanity will become a huge megablur of clones. Wasn't it Qoheleth who suggested, "For everything there is a season and a time for every matter under heaven"? We must deny the urge to ask all people to conform to any predetermined standard. A balanced world needs people of all types, mutually committed to coexistence.

This was the message in Paul's analysis in I Corinthians 12 of the church as the body of Christ. Please note, the Apostle did not suggest everyone try to be the same. To the contrary, he underscored interdependence among divergent pieces.

For the body does not consist of one member but of many. If the foot should say, "Because I am not a hand, I do not belong to the body," that would not make it any less a part of the body. And if the ear should say, "Because I am not an eye, I do not belong to the body," that would not make it any less a part of the body. If the whole body were an eye, where would be the hearing? If the whole body were an ear, where would be the sense of smell? But as it is, God arranged the organs in the body, each one of them, as he chose. If all were a single organ, where would the body be? As it is, there are many parts, yet one body. (I Corinthians 12:14-20)

As I study the unrest in South Africa, observe the widening distance between the social classes in America, and sense the growth of Islam around the world, I recognize the increasing need for interdependence. Midst all the chaos, one theme keeps resurfacing: *We need each other.*

Children of hope do not question that truth. They sense there is a place for people of color, women, homosexuals, and other oppressed people at the front of humanity's bus, teaching and leading blind bigots to see the Christ in every person.

A STONE MESSAGE

Labradorite is a type of crystal that, at first glance, appears totally worthless. A child collecting stones would most likely cast it aside as a chunk of coal. Nevertheless, those who examine it closely will find it hauntingly beautiful. Rotated in the light, there is a point where Labradorite sparkles with every color in the rainbow.

I believe God created human beings with the same attribute. Hence, if we are to choose hope and help the oppressed do the same, our first assignment is to lift

116

them to the light of acceptance so as to reflect their fullest value.

Henri Nouwen encountered this truth during his sojourn in South America. During his stay, a fellow priest handed him a list of requests prepared by a Third World bishop for all who would be missionaries in that oppressed area. The list would be applauded by all who are shackled by unjust systems. It must be heeded by all who would impart hope.

Help us discover our own riches; don't judge us poor because we lack what you have.

type of shackles you wear.

Be patient with us as a people; don't judge us backward simply because we don't follow your stride.

Be patient with our pace; don't judge us lazy simply because we can't follow your tempo.

Be patient with our symbols; don't judge us ignorant because we can't read your signs.

Be with us and proclaim the richness of your life which you can share with us.

Be with us and be open to what we can give.

Be with us as a companion who walks with us . . . neither behind nor in front . . . in search for life and ultimately for God!

(*Gracias!* [New York: Harper & Row, 1983], p. 22)

We enable hope by affirming innate value, not by dominating with power and judgment but by cultivating with love and understanding. I really believe this was behind the Lord's gripping analogy of the log and the speck in Matthew 7. Let's face it, most of us don't try to understand either issues or persons over which we have total control. Oh, but how well those who are under control manage to understand their oppressors. Experience tells me, sad but true, that employees understand bosses better than bosses understand employees, that blacks understand whites better than whites understand blacks, that women understand men better than men understand women, and that gays understand straights better than straights understand gays.

Why? Because domination has a blinding effect. Albeit mistaken, the most common assumption of people of power is that they really don't need the people underneath them. On the other hand, the oppressed are all too aware of the need to understand those who hold them down. It's the only way they can survive.

I think of George Jean Nathan's telltale observance, "Women's famous intuition is only man's transparency." Having coped with male dominance for centuries, it is no surprise that women have learned to read men's moods, anticipate their desires, and manage their blindness. Meanwhile man, ensconced in a tower of power, labels woman an enigma, thereby avoiding the challenge to understand and bypassing the treasure of interdependence.

THE CALL TO CULTIVATE

Cultivation, the method of Christ and the seedbed of hope, is another matter altogether. Domination divides. Cultivation blends.

Hal Lyon underlines the promise of strength when bigotry is conquered: "In trees strength takes the form of sturdy branches, deep roots, and many leaves. In a relationship, it may take the form of a powerful blending that allows the individuals involved to experience what strength feels like when it is *added* to strength" (*Tenderness Is Strength* [New York: Harper & Row, 1977], p. 25; italics added).

Thus, the message that must be communicated to

the oppressed is how deeply they are needed. Whereas some may think the world would do just fine without blacks, gays, and women in business, only a fool would not recognize how much the quality of life has been positively affected by these people. Apart from their influence, all hope is short-lived.

So the challenge to affirm all and reject none is apparent. As the world shrinks, we are destined to discover that there are no little people. Whenever I think about this issue, my mind runs to a story told by Arthur Tennies.

I remember reading during the Korean War about a misfit inductee. He soon became the butt of all the jokes in his training platoon. The sergeant, a veteran of the war, soon became disgusted with this useless excuse for a soldier and made his life hell. One day the men in his platoon decided to play a clever joke on him. A dummy grenade was obtained. The sergeant told the platoon that it was a live grenade. He handed it to one of the inductees to throw. The inductee pulled the pin and fumbled with it, letting it drop at the feet of the misfit. Quick as a flash the misfit fell on the grenade, burying it in his stomach. As the seconds ticked by, he slowly realized it was all a joke. He had made an ass of himself again. In humiliation he finally looked up. But no one was laughing. The sergeant slowly helped the misfit to his feet and carefully dusted him off. Never again did anyone laugh at the misfit's bumbling. The fool was willing to die for those who ridiculed him. (*A Church for Sinners, Seekers, and Sundry Non-Saints* [Nashville: Abingdon, 1974], p. 86)

Little people? There is no such thing.

As one whose faith centers in the life of a misfit, I am increasingly sensitive to those of our society who either cannot or will not conform to the expectations of the masses. If I am fortunate, I will learn how to affirm and understand them. If so, my hope and theirs will increase.

I think Christ's record is relatively clear in this area. He saw a seed of promise in every human being. Confronted by oppressed people, whether tax collectors or centurions, Gentiles or Jews, prostitutes or politicians, his response was predictable: acceptance, affirmation, and unconditional love.

POWER FROM UNEXPECTED SOURCES

Consider the million-dollar lunch break that took place in Cincinnati back in 1878. It involved an hourly wage earner at Proctor & Gamble. On paper, and according to the company flow chart, this guy was a nobody. He manned the stirring vats for a product identified only as "white soap." It was a pleasant product, carefully perfumed and delicately balanced. Were it not for the lunch break in question, it would have been one among many, just another soap.

On this particular occasion, our hero, to this day nameless, must have had a very important noon encounter, for he left in such a hurry that he neglected to turn off the mixers. Upon his return, he was shocked to find his vats filled with over-mixed soap, nearly bubbling onto the floor. Rather than admit his error, he poured the soap into the hardening and cutting frames and the batch was subsequently released to nearby stores. Within three weeks, the Proctor & Gamble switchboard lit up with requests. America had fallen in love with "the soap that floats." In 1979, Ivory enjoyed its one hundredth birthday, with over thirty-two billion cakes sold.

The point? In an interdependent world there are no little people. Everybody makes a difference, even the vat man who forgets to shut down the mixers. The march of progress consistently hinges on nondescript individuals who, often unawares, make life-changing contributions to society.

Hence, if we are to impart the gift of hope to the oppressed, we must make a practice of empowering the powerless.

I think of an incident from the late sixties involving the arrogance of the Daley administration in Chicago. As I recall, the city was about to condemn an entire block of low-income property to appropriate the land for a city project. When the people of the neighborhood approached City Hall, the mayor wouldn't even talk to them. They were powerless nobodies, or so the authorities thought, and so the people believed, until they made contact with Saul Alinsky. The late social activist suggested the neighborhood leaders organize their friends, charter a dozen buses, and head for O'Hare Airport, "hizzoner's" pride and joy. Once inside the terminal, they used a power they never knew they had. En masse, they occupied every public relief station in the place. Within a few hours, they had their conference with Richard J. Daley and negotiated an acceptable arrangement for the property in question.

The challenge is to empower oppressed people where they are, to show them what they already have.

THE BIBLICAL PRECEDENT

This is precisely what took place at Pentecost. The Master was gone. Twelve regular, befuddled, somewhat intimidated human beings were left to wrap the world with his love. The task seemed impossible. But nothing is impossible under the guidance of the Holy Spirit. Through the Holy Spirit, Jesus Christ meets us at the point of need. "When the day of Pentecost had come, they were all together in one place. And suddenly a sound came from heaven like the rush of a mighty wind . . . and there appeared to them tongues as of fire . . . and they began to speak in other tongues, as the Spirit gave them utterance" (Acts 2:1-4).

When the need was clear, the powerless were empowered. It can happen again.

The last few years have been particularly tough for the poor. As the rhetoric of war has increased, they have watched defense spending skyrocket, while resources for the oppressed have steadily dwindled. Worse yet, the word has gone forth that Lyndon Johnson's Great Society efforts were meaningless.

In November 1980, a CBS–*New York Times* national poll found that 62 percent of the public believed the antipoverty programs of the sixties either had had little impact on the poor or had made things worse for them. The current administration supports that view, indicating that since 1960 "there has been a steady increase in the level of poverty right up to the present," in spite of government social aid programs.

But the facts tell us something different. Indeed, there is a great deal of waste and misuse in the American poverty program, but in spite of its blemishes it has been extraordinarily effective. A recent *Washington Post* article explains that a much smaller percentage of Americans live below the poverty level today than when the effort to attack the problem began some twenty years ago. In 1965, 17.3 percent of our population qualified as victims of poverty. In 1982, in spite of the rage of inflation during the interim, only 15 percent fell in that category.

The article went on to explain what would happen if all government benefits were removed. In that case, the rate in 1965 would have been 21.3 percent and the rate in 1982 would have been 24 percent. In other words, without aid from the government, nearly one-fourth of the people in the most prosperous nation on earth would be living in poverty. So the record is clear, empowering the powerless is an American tradition, a tradition which must not be scrapped on behalf of an already superior military program. Yes, we must keep pace with our adversaries. But let us not forget that poverty qualifies in that category.

Johann Goethe put the challenge this way: "If you treat a person as he is, he will stay as he is; but if you treat him as he ought to be and could be, he will become what he ought to be and could be."

Choosing hope means choosing the poor and oppressed. It means recognizing the potential of the individual—in the classroom and on the street, in the boardroom and on the loading dock, in the university and in the ghetto.

POWER BARS

Frequently, I am called to New York to work with the Board for Homeland Ministries of the United Church of Christ. During one such trip I found myself strolling out of the lobby of a Manhattan hotel at one o'clock in the morning. The rest of my colleagues had gone to bed, but I could not sleep. The city was quiet. I could hear my footsteps as I walked. Occasionally, a truck would creak around a corner, or a horn would blare, or a person I did not know would shout some indecipherable message to someone else I did not know. Surrounded by millions of human beings, I felt very much alone in my journey. In a strange sense, time seemed to freeze as I walked, as if I were being given a second chance to examine an issue I had overlooked.

Then I became sensitive to them—the bars. Not the good-time kind, but the steel kind. Every window was scissored with them. Every door.

I slowed my gait to peer through the ghastly barriers. I saw stereos. I saw motorbikes. I saw designer shirts and designer jeans. I saw computers. And then I saw something that brought me hard against reality. I saw food. It must have been some kind of warehouse. The skids were piled high with cardboard boxes; some said Kellogg's, others said Campbell's. I've known the names since I was a kid. Now, they had new meaning. Now, they told me staples are luxuries to some folk. They need to be locked up. Like all the electronic goodies next door, food would bring a good price on the street.

I thought, "The bars are there to discourage criminals, not poor people." Right. But there is a more pertinent message. You see, the bars are not there for you or me. We can lay hold of such bounty whenever we wish. The bars can't stop us because we can buy what we want. The real power of those bars is in our indifference to them. It is an indifference all too often duplicated when we are confronted with the poor and oppressed. Their problems are not our problems. Their bars are not our bars.

If we are to choose hope, this must change.

PERSPECTIVE ON PRIORITIES

When Colin Morris, then president of the United Church in Zambia, opened the mail box, he felt a twinge of excitement. On top of everything sat the latest edition of *The Methodist Recorder*, with a front page article about the proposed merger between the Anglican Church and the Methodist Church. Things were not going smoothly. Debates raged over communion forms, organizational structure, the role of the bishops, and the appointment process by which ministers and churches were tied together.

Morris liked that kind of thing. Truth is, he had contributed a few pungent articles himself, just to fan the flames. Now, he smiled. The church was being the church: praying and preying, splitting into factions, cloaking personal preference with theological jargon.

Walking back to the house, he spotted the body out of the corner of his eye. At first it looked like a clump of rags, but as he turned to investigate, he knew it was a human being. Kneeling, he examined the little old man for a pulse. There was none.

Later in the day, the autopsy report confirmed Morris's suspicions and changed his life. The pathologist said the elderly Zambian had died of hunger. In his shrunken stomach were a few leaves and what appeared to be a ball of grass. Nothing else.

Considering the church newspaper and the autopsy report side by side, Colin Morris decided his energies had been misplaced. He proceeded to write a book entitled *Include Me Out!* which has shaped opinions for

In a world where half a billion people are starving, in a nation where social aid programs have been and will be reduced by billions of dollars, in a state with over one million people living below the poverty level, and on the fringe of a neighborhood where the average annual income is in excess of $43,000, I am perplexed, challenged, and confused by poverty. How can we instill hope in people who have no idea whence cometh their next meal?

A DOUBLE–EDGED ISSUE

In the nineteenth chapter of the book of Leviticus, in the earlier portion of what the Jews called "the Holiness Code," we read:

125

When you reap the harvest of your land, you shall not reap your field to its very border, neither shall you gather the gleanings after your harvest. And you shall not strip your vineyard bare, neither shall you gather the fallen grapes of your vineyard; you shall leave them for the poor and for the sojourner: I am the Lord your God. (Leviticus 19:9-10)

With those words, Moses was reminding his people of the faithfulness of God and the ever-present mandate to share their blessings. He was also pointing to the root of poverty: dualism. You see, if we didn't have wealth, we wouldn't have poverty. Relative terms, one depends on the other. And when Christians get serious about extending the blessings of hope to the poor and oppressed, we need to start by recognizing this dualism as the heart of the matter.

What is dualism? It is the process of seeing things as either/or, black/white, always divided. With regard to poverty, it is a matter of the "haves" and the "have-nots." There is a nebulous line between the two. The customs, power bases, and social structures determining whether one is in one class or the other are major contributors to the existence of poverty in a world with more than enough resources to supply its people.

One of the abiding problems of dealing with poverty involves the emotional charge the issue carries at both ends of the spectrum. When poor folks talk poverty, they flush with anger at those who need an explanation to understand. On the other hand, when wealthy people—and on a relative basis, that is what most of us are—talk poverty, we stiffen with resistance about a problem we not only don't have, but prefer not to recognize.

Please note, Moses did not assault his people because they owned the fields; he simply ordered them to share the bounty. Ownership is not the issue, indifference is. In my opinion, it is no sin to be prosperous. It is a terrible sin to be prosperously indifferent.

It is John who quoted the Master, "The poor you will always have with you." As I deal with my congregation, I sometimes think we take that phrase as an excuse to forget about an unsolvable problem. To the contrary, I see it as a reminder of an ongoing responsibility. I don't believe we should ever feel guilty about prosperity. On the other hand, I hope we shall always feel guilty about not caring for those less fortunate than ourselves.

A SELF–PERPETUATING PROBLEM

The problem with dualism is the subtle manner in which it perpetuates itself. Blessed with wealth, we begin to think it is more important than it really is. Consequently, we soon find ourselves captured and controlled by the symptoms of the condition. Here, sin materializes.

Having tasted the comforts of affluence, we go a step further and embrace symbol at the expense of substance. To invest unnecessary resources in an effort to remind others of social position is, indeed, a reinforcing of dualism and an insult to the poor. If the primary purpose in purchasing a Mercedes rather than a Chevrolet is to impress others, the extra expense is ethically questionable. However, if the motivation is a matter of affordable quality and long-term investment, it may be a wise and thoughtful deed. Tragedy strikes when we get so immersed in affluence that we confuse need with privilege. The first is a matter of survival. The second is a measure of blessing.

Annie Dillard underscores the danger when she writes about the Franklin Expedition, which set out to find the northwest passage across the Canadian Arctic to the Pacific Ocean in 1845. They failed and died. What is worse is the manner in which it happened. Twenty years after their ill-fated effort, a search party found the remains of those who had gone forth on foot after the main ship was immobilized. The bounty found with the skeletons betrayed a sick, all too familiar value system: silver tea sets, an ivory backgammon board, hundreds of pounds of silver flatware, and a pocket filled with gold letter clips. It wasn't the last time the trappings of prestige and wealth would cost human beings their lives.

When I think about poverty, this is where I get a yank in my stomach. I do not begrudge the finer things in life; I enjoy them as much as anyone. Still, confronted with the question, What's the difference between stainless steel and silver spoons? I squirm.

Dualism is the culprit. It reinforces questionable values. It also traps us with either/or definitions. Frankly, our world is traumatized by overemphasized differences between the old and the young, urban and rural, conservative and liberal, wealthy and poor. Such lines serve only to separate people and dilute the level of our living. I count it a mark of God's grace that technology is blurring the differences. The gap between the old and the young is narrowing. The arbitrary conservative/liberal split is significant only to those at the furthest extremes. And the most meaningful variance between the wealthy and the poor might dissolve with but a moderate effort from the people at the top.

Choosing hope, not only for ourselves but for the oppressed as well, means intentionally enabling that effort.

Matthew Fox specifically confronts this issue. He sees the hope of civilization in a concentrated emphasis on similarities as opposed to differences. "I believe that the truly adult spiritual journey is precisely this: a journey from dualism to dialectic. From Either/Or to Both/And. Until people can make such a journey they are incapable of compassion" (*A Spirituality Named Compassion and the Healing of the Global Village, Humpty Dumpty and Us* [Minneapolis: Winston, 1979], p. 84).

Moses said, "Leave some food in the field; don't pretend the poor do not exist; fall not victim to the narcissism that denies the existence of anyone but yourself." But that's hard to do in a world dominated by consumerism. The "haves" can afford to have more. So we do. And with every acquisition, the gap between the prosperous and the poor expands.

The question remains, DO WE NEED IT? And, if we don't need it, is the wisest expenditure of privilege that which widens the gap between the wealthy and the poor, that which squashes the hope of the oppressed?

We are called to share, proportionately, the blessings God has given. The more we have, the more we share. It's that simple.

FREE FROM THINGS

Does the word "glutton" make any sense at this point? Webster tells us a glutton is "one given to habitually greedy and voracious eating and drinking." It seems to me this would be the person who gleaned everything from the field. This would be the insidious creature who takes all for himself while staring incredulously at those in need. This would be the family with an income four or five times the national poverty level, yet so caught up in the world of things that they cannot, or will not, set aside a percentage for the poor and the sojourner.

Here, the words of Meister Eckhart drift into consciousness: "There where our clinging to things ends, is where God begins to be."

Thus, yet another influence of dualism appears. If the plight of the poor is determined by the practice of the wealthy, our greed is another's need.

When we overindulge because we have the power to do so, we force others to underindulge because they have no power to avoid it. Poverty can be traced to the affluent, not because of what we have but because of the way we use it. Plenty and power are intertwined; the one reinforces the other.

Agronomists tell us there is enough food to feed the world, plus. It's the system of distribution that is at fault. Hence the practice of restraint on behalf of the "haves" combined with an intentionally balanced method of apportionment for the "have-nots" stand as a logical approach to restoring hope to the oppressed.

Recall with me that fabulous incident from the twelfth chapter of Mark, where Jesus stations himself in the Temple to observe the contributions of the people. One by one, they file past the treasury making their contributions. He noted the people who gave enough to be respectable, and it didn't excite him much. Now and again, a heavy hitter would plunk some gold into the plate, and the treasurer would smile approval. The Master showed no emotion until a ragged widow toddled up and clunked down two copper coins. Suddenly, Christ was on his feet. He called to the disciples. There was a message here he did not want them to miss. "Truly, I say to you, this poor widow has put in more than all those who are contributing to the treasury. For they all contributed out of their abundance; but she out of her poverty has put in everything she had, her whole living" (Matthew 12:43-44).

It is no wonder he loved such a gift; he was to make one just like it at Golgotha. Furthermore, it was a clear illustration of the total commitment he expects from all of us. Our hope flourishes because of his actions. The hope of the oppressed can flourish if we will follow his example.

I find it hard to misconstrue the message. People who really care do not make contributions on the basis of interest earned. People who really care make contributions which touch the principle. For them, giving is not a matter of doing what is respectable. Rather, for people who really care, giving is a matter of faithful response to what God has first given them.

Let me conclude this chapter with an anecdote borrowed from World War II. Before the Allies landed on D-Day, they used a form of saturation bombing to pummel the coast of Normandy. In the process the little village of Cherbourg was flattened.

Cherbourg had been a peasant's village; most of the people there earned their living from the soil. A proud folk, they had joined together to build their own church. The bombs annihilated it.

When the war concluded, the people of Cherbourg decided to rebuild their church. They sifted through the wreckage seeking to save anything salvageable. They were particularly interested in a hand-carved crucifix that had graced the chancel. Through many days, they painstakingly pieced the work of art together, only to discover that the tips of the cross, bearing the hands of the Master, were missing. Since the original artist had been killed near the end of the war, they found it necessary to place an ad in trade papers all over the continent, seeking an artist to repair their crucifix.

Six months passed before the first response. The artist arrived, looked at the crucifix, and turned down the job—"It just wouldn't look right." A few weeks later, another craftsman offered the same assessment. Finally, after a year of waiting, the peasants sensed a different message.

Today, if you were to visit that little church, you would see a sign hanging around the neck of our Lord. It carries a message for every person who sincerely desires to overcome poverty: "Christ has no hands but ours."

6

Hope and Tragedy

IT CAN HAPPEN TO ANYBODY

Stewart Alsop served his country in World War II, met and married a British girl with whom he raised a fine family, wrote for *Newsweek* magazine, and at about 9:30 in the morning on July 19, 1971—having dumped a load of garbage into an old well at the family homestead in Maryland—found himself immobilized. He was gasping for breath, his heart thumping so hard he could hear it.

That afternoon, doctors told him he was suffering from acute myeloblastic leukemia. The prognosis: a 50 percent chance of living a year, twenty to one for two years. Chances of a cure were statistically negligible.

Alsop lived for more than four years and in the interim wrote *Stay of Execution*, a captivating account of a decent man clinging to life, befriending death, and trying to make sense of the visit of misfortune.

It couldn't be done, and that is where this chapter finds it's focus. How do we choose hope in the midst of disaster? Tragedy has no respect for persons. If it did, noble persons would not die young, children would be immune to disease, cancer would be but a northern zodiacal constellation, lightning would never hit a human being, and tornados would courteously avoid the structures of civilization.

But we all know better. Tragedy is a fact of life, and for those who believe in a God of love, it fosters some very difficult questions. Why do innocent human beings perish in airplane crashes? Why does crime visit its ugliness on children? Why do people who have made a life of helping others conclude their lives in sterile isolation? Why do hands of love gnarl under the influence of arthritis? Why is there rape, murder, cystic fibrosis, and terrorism?

OUR CAUSE–AND–EFFECT WORLD

We must begin our response to these questions with the observation that the existence of a loving God does not preclude the laws of cause and effect. The Creator structured the world with two fixed influences: the laws of nature and the nature of humanity. The first is predictably consistent, the second consistently un-predictable.

Gravity is a law of nature. It performs with alarming consistency and it has absolutely no respect for persons. A penny dropped from atop the Sears Tower in Chicago will fall at the same rate of speed as one dropped from the Eiffel Tower in Paris. Furthermore, that penny will not alter its course to accommodate the persons on the sidewalk below. If either Harold Washington or François Mitterand were to walk underneath that plummeting penny, he would be thumped with the same intensity as a city street worker.

When dealing with the laws of nature, we make a mistake if we assume moral, ethical, or spiritual attributes hold any influence. I refuse to believe Dag

Hammarskjöld deserved to die in an airplane in the jungles of Africa in 1961. I cannot reconcile the untimely death of Martin Luther King, Jr., with the liberating work he was doing in 1968. And it makes no sense to me that Hubert Humphrey would be ravaged by cancer.

These were all fine human beings, doing their best to make this world a better place to live. But ours is a cause-and-effect world. When an aluminum flying machine traveling in excess of one hundred miles per hour smashes into a tree, the occupants of the machine are in great jeopardy. When a psychotic human being fires a rifle bullet through the throat of a prophet, the prophet is in great jeopardy. And when the cells of a human activist's body go out of control, generating tumors which compress vital organs, the activist is in great jeopardy.

You say, "Yes, but what about providence? And what about justice? Isn't God in charge?" Yes and no. Ultimately, yes. For the temporal moment we know as life, no.

LIFE, A BOOK WITH TWO CHAPTERS

Perhaps an analogy will clarify the issue. Let us hypothetically assume the Creator designed *The Book of Life* with two chapters. The first, life between the point of conception and the instant of death, includes every word ever conceived but is relatively short compared to the second chapter, eternal life in the presence of God. Looking upon the first chapter, the Author decided to share it with some beloved friends, you and me and all of humanity. In fact, it was surrendered to us to do with as we pleased. To be sure, we are free to rewrite, but we are constrained to use only the original content. We cannot create. We can add nothing. We can only reshape what is here.

This is where the excitement starts. As we maneuver the words, some of us create poetry, some prose, some epics of pain, and some sonnets of love. We do as we please, and we live with the consequences. Governed by grammatical laws, we are in charge for a while, but only in chapter 1, and even then, our deeds and decisions are valid only in that chapter.

Then comes chapter 2. It has no end. It belongs to the Creator. And the only clue to its content was revealed when the Creator sent forth a Son to share the adventure in chapter 1. Noting that we had fouled up the story, the Sovereign One shared the Son to give us a glimpse of how to do it right. But we didn't appreciate the counsel and wrote the Son out of the manuscript.

Here's the clue. He came back, for two reasons: to underscore the temporal nature of chapter 1 and to point our souls toward a higher plane of living in anticipation of chapter 2. We live in chapter 1. God waits with chapter 2. Hope occupies the space in between.

As we go about shaping our world, we are bound by time and content, as God has foreordained. What we do with both is up to us. Still, the life, death, and resurrection of Jesus Christ stand as a permanent reminder that there is more to come. Only when we enter that realm will the laws of cause and effect give way to the law of perfect peace.

TEMPORARY TRAUMA

Hence, in attempting to choose hope in the midst of pain and tragedy, we are wise to note that such conditions are temporal at best. Disaster can strike. It

cannot prevail. Cancer can flourish. It cannot survive.
War can erupt. It cannot persist. Pain can paralyze. It
cannot endure.

C. S. Lewis specifically addressed this concern in his
cogent little book, *The Problem of Pain*.

> So it is with the life of souls in a world; fixed laws,
> consequences unfolding by causal necessity, the whole
> natural order, are at once the limits within which their
> common life is confined and also the sole condition under
> which any such life is possible. Try to exclude the possibility
> of suffering which the order of nature and the existence of
> free-will involve, and you find that you have excluded life
> itself. ([London: Fontana Books, 1957], p. 22)

The most difficult aspect of this line of reasoning for
me is the concept of justice. I brushed it briefly when I
referred earlier to tragedy in the lives of good people.
Obviously, what is deserved and what actually takes
place are rarely harmonious. That makes me angry,
frustrated, and confused.

My attitude shifts when I recall the Passion of
Christ. If ever one did not deserve to suffer, it was our
Lord. Still, as one fully subject to the parameters of
chapter 1, he ran the same risk that every human being
must endure.

Frederick Buechner helps us accept our pain when
he reminds us of that of the Master. He points to the
biting symbolism of the Russian Orthodox cross. You
will remember it includes two pieces generally
omitted from other crosses. The one at the top
represents the mental anguish of Christ, manifested in
the sign placed above his head reading "King of the
Jews" in Hebrew, Latin, and Greek. His murderers
wanted his humiliation to be complete. The one at the
bottom is a slanted board. It is the platform, always
present, on which crucified prisoners were to stand to

keep from ripping free from the nails. This piece was positioned just a few inches beneath the feet so as to keep the tension on the hanging points while still providing support. It vividly illustrates the inhumanity of humans to humans. The slant? It developed when the victim, in a moment of wrenching pain, pressed down with one foot. Hard.

Is there a more lucid reminder that this world, the same world once graced with the physical presence of God, is a cause-and-effect world?

EXCEPTIONS TO THE RULE

But sometimes such logical progressions are interrupted. Sometimes God witnesses the mess in chapter 1 and intervenes. Sometimes, there are miracles!

Lazarus is called forth from the tomb. The blind receive sight. A hemorrhaging woman is healed. The lame walk. The dumb speak. The deaf hear. Tumors disappear. And when these developments occur they defy explanation.

At this point, I want to endorse the power of God in the Holy Spirit. I believe the Holy Spirit can turn a person into a grapefruit if God so wills. I believe the Holy Spirit is an ever-present, unquenchable source of power capable of breaking the laws of cause and effect whenever God so desires.

And there's the catch. Miracles are the bailiwick of the Almighty and have nothing to do with the lifestyle of the human beings involved. We can't earn them. We can't demand them. We can't pray them into reality. And we can't buy them. Like life itself, miracles are unmerited gifts from God.

I am deeply concerned about the style of faith that presumes the right to barter with the Creator. "I've been faithful to you, Lord, now you be faithful to me."

"If I have enough faith, God will heal me." "If God is love, my suffering will cease!"

All such thought presumes a degree of leverage which human beings simply do not possess. We are not co-equals with God. We cannot manipulate divine power—not with good, not with evil, not with public displays, and not with private agony.

Again, Lewis makes the point: "The problem of reconciling human suffering with the existence of a God who loves, is only insoluble so long as we attach a trivial meaning to the word 'love,' and look at things as if man were the centre of them. Man is not the centre. God does not exist for the sake of man" (*The Problem of Pain*, p. 36).

THE SOURCE OF OUR HOPE

The source of our hope in the midst of tragedy is the resurrection. In conquering death, Jesus Christ revealed the ultimate will of God, which is eternal peace. Our knowledge of that event enables us to surrender our will to God's will, to choose hope, and to rise above disaster. I can be hopeful no matter what the situation, because I believe in ultimate peace with God.

Recall with me the agony of our Lord in the Garden of Gethsemane. Truth is, Christ liked chapter 1. Just like you and me, he loved life. He enjoyed his friends. He took strength from the beauty of the dawn and the silence of the night. I'm sure he thoroughly enjoyed fishing with Peter, debating with John, analyzing with Thomas. But now the laws of cause and effect were painting an ugly picture. The end was at hand.

So what did he do? He identified his will and surrendered to God's. "Father, if it be possible, let this cup pass from me. Nevertheless, not my will, but Thine be done!"

SURRENDERING TO PEACE

I believe the will to which our Lord was referring had nothing to do with the cross. Christ was not crediting the Creator for the coming crucifixion. In the cause and effect world of chapter 1, that was a matter of inevitable consequence. No, the will to which our Lord was submitting was God's ultimate will, namely, the peace of eternity.

That peace can be claimed in this lifetime. And when it is, we, like Christ, rise above the pain of temporal condition and find meaning and strength in its promise. Suffer? Yes, we still suffer. So did he. We feel the pain. So did he. We experience the loss. So did he. We know the hurt, the emptiness, and the isolation. And so did he. But we also know, as did the Master, the ultimate victory is ours, and therein is the strength to overcome—not somehow, but triumphantly.

Recall with me that great narrative from the book of Genesis. Remember the record of the disaster? The whole earth has been flooded. All life, save that of Noah, his family, and a menagerie of animals, has been snuffed out. Can you imagine? Just think of the loneliness, the eerie sense of an erased past, the challenge of starting again, and the abiding fear of a God who would allow such a thing to happen.

In every direction, the man of God could see nothing but water. His vision, his hope, his power to reason were caput. He, as a finite human being, did not have the power to conquer the situation.

Still, choosing hope, Noah released a dove to search for land. But the Bible says that dove "found no place to set her foot" and returned. In effect, poor old Noah had symbolically placed a call to God, only to be put on "hold."

So he sent out the dove a second time. And what a moment it must have been when the old man saw the gentle creature winging her way homeward, and, as she hurtled out of the sky, noted for the first time *a freshly plucked olive leaf* in her mouth.

He could not see the land, but he knew it was there.

This, then, is the ongoing promise to those who choose hope, to those who are mired in the grip of pain, to those who are decimated by the laws of nature, and to those who know the hollow hallways of isolation, tragedy, and immeasurable hurt. From within the chaotic indifference of chapter 1, we cannot see the land, but in Christ we find a freshly plucked olive leaf pointing toward a day when all tragedy shall be overcome and all pain destroyed.

THE ROAD TO HOPE

As our Lord was delivering the Sermon on the Mount, he gazed at all the intent faces before him and set out the summons that would separate the children of hope from the children of despair: "Enter by the narrow gate; for the gate is wide and the way is easy, that leads to destruction, and those who enter by it are many. For the gate is narrow and the way is hard, that leads to life and those who find it are few" (Matthew 7:13-14).

Those of us who would choose hope in the midst of tragedy will be very familiar with the narrow gate. It is much easier to complain of unfair treatment. It is much easier to question the justice of God. It is much easier to blame others and slip into self-centered despair. But what is easy and what is faithful rarely coincide.

I think of the parlor game "Labyrinth." You will recall it involves a wooden box with two knobs located on the sides, one in front, the other on the right. The knobs control the slant of playing surface, which is a maze pierced by multiple holes. The object is to maneuver a steel bearing through the maze, avoiding the holes, using only the knobs to determine direction and speed of the ball. It is a frustrating and fascinating game. If you go too fast the bearing clunks through a hole; if you go too slow, it doesn't move at all. The skilled player soon learns the secret of maintaining tension on each of the knobs and thereby mastering the destiny of the bearing.

Narrow gate people know a similar secret. Though the way may be difficult, they maintain tension between the demands of the world and the commands of God, thereby establishing a balanced, yet disciplined, approach to decisions. Better yet, as children of hope, they have no fear of the holes—the pressure situations, the high risk decisions. For after all, if they fall through, they know the Master will pick them up and help them start again.

SMALL RISK, GREAT OPPORTUNITY

The challenge for the achiever is to recognize that one can't avoid the holes without assistance from the Lord. So often, having established a degree of control over our well-being, we make the erroneous assumption that we did it on our own, that we hold both knobs. Wrong. Everything we have is channeled through Jesus' grace. If he didn't want us to have it, it would not be ours. Even so, when we take inventory of our blessings, we should fall on our knees in gratitude.

God has been very good to us. We live in the finest country in the history of civilization. We are free to pursue happiness with little government restraint and full religious liberty. We are privileged to have the best life-support systems on the face of the earth: hospitals, schools, research centers, and churches. We have ample food, extravagant shelter, phenomenal mobility, and endless sources of entertainment. And, perhaps most significantly, we are surrounded by opportunity. Whatever we can conceive, we can achieve, if we have the patience and faith to wait upon the Lord.

This is the legacy of hope. Through faith, all things are possible, even the defeat of death.

But the way is not easy.

KEY LINK: COURAGE AND HOPE

The assumption that affluence and peace are synonymous is false. One can command an empire yet die in search of the soul. Peace comes only from a daily cognizance of Christ's presence, a hand in hand, day by day, decision by decision friendship. And from that peace issues a courage that abides.

Courage isn't a brilliant flash,
A daring deed in a moment's flash;
It isn't an instantaneous thing
Born of despair with a sudden spring
It isn't a creature of flickered hope
Or the final tug at a slipping rope;
But it's something deep in the soul of a man
That is working always to serve some plan.
Courage isn't the last resort

In the work of life or the game of sport;
It isn't a thing that a person can call
At some future time when apt to fall;
If one hasn't it now, one will have it not
When the strain is great and the pace is hot.
For who would strive for a distant goal
Must always have courage within the soul.
Courage isn't a dazzling light
That flashes and passes away from sight;
it's a slow, unwavering, ingrained trait
With the patience to work and the strength to wait
                              (Edgar Guest, "Courage")

Courage, in this context, issues from a constant sense of God's presence combined with an uncanny awareness of the proper time to act. We are not here by chance. Courageous persons know that. They know they have a purpose, a calling beyond the self, a unique responsibility to decide and act.

Søren Kierkegaard called this point the "leap of faith." It's that point of commitment more dependent on projection than on proof. Human beings are simply not capable of having all the answers. Hence, those who would grow take many a step, even in the midst of tragedy, not knowing exactly what comes next.

I find it fascinating how the paranoid human mind focuses immediately on the "narrow gate" of Christ's teaching. The first issue is not the gate. It's the decision to enter!

We are called to move, to act, to make a commitment, to take a risk, to forge into new territory, trusting God to effect the consequences.

Can you imagine where we would be if Christ had demanded proof of the resurrection before complying with the crucifixion?

But Christ did not demand an airtight deal before he

made his commitment. And even when things appeared to be the worst, when the crowds jeered his retching body and mocked his apparent impotence, even then, with his last breath he trusted the future to God. "Father, into Thy hands I commit my Spirit."

DECLARATIONS AND DEEDS

In 1859, ten thousand people gathered to watch a man die at Niagara Falls. Jean Francois Gravelet, a French tightrope walker known in this country as Charles Blondin, had promised to cross the roaring falls on a high wire. It was a foolhardy promise. The gusting winds and constant vapor from the falls made such a promise absolutely untenable.

Betting odds were not directed on whether or not he would make it; rather, bookies were covering bets on where he would fall. The 1,100-foot cable glistened in the morning sun, as Blondin took the first step. The crowd hushed. For the first three hundred feet he seemed awkward, hesitant, almost like he didn't believe he was there. But, then, somewhere around the five hundred foot mark, his confidence rallied. For the last half of his perilous journey, the thunderous sound of the falls was punctuated by the unison shouts of the inspired crowd: "Blondin! Blondin! Blondin!"

Reaching the American side, he acknowledged their cheers and picked up a megaphone. "You did not believe I could make it. Now you cheer. Do you believe I can return carrying a person on my back?"

As one, they responded. "We believe! We believe! We believe!"

Again, he acknowledged their adoration and picked

up the megaphone. "Of course you believe. Now, who will volunteer to be that person?"

Twenty thousand eyes stared at the ground. Then, after a minute which lasted an hour, one man raised his hand. He climbed onto Blondin's shoulders and allowed him to carry him back across the wire to the Canadian side of the falls.

Writes Anthony Campolo about this incident:

> Ten thousand people had cried, "We believe, we believe, we believe." But in the end, only one really believed. Belief is more than just intellectual assent to propositional statements about reality. Believing is dangerously and radically giving yourself over to that in which you believe, without any evidence to assure that you have decided rightly. (*A Reasonable Faith* [Waco, Tx.: Word, 1983], p. 106)

That's the leap of faith apart from which no gate is ever entered and no life is ever changed. It is choosing hope.

COPING NOW

So, apart from trusting in the ultimate promise of God, how are we to cope with the visit of tragedy?

Robert Veninga lists four characteristics of people who survive tragedy. They are worth noting as we conclude this chapter.

1. Almost without exception those who survive a tragedy give credit to one person who stood by them, supported them, and gave them a sense of hope. . . .
2. Those who survive a tragedy understand the magnitude of that which they have lost. . . .
3. Those who survive a tragedy have learned to transcend their guilt. . . .
4. If you want to survive a crisis, you need a reason to live.
   (*A Gift of Hope*, pp. 60-77)

I choose not to get involved here with lengthy explanations of those points. Veninga does a marvelous job in his book. Rather, I would like to apply those points to a situation with which almost all of us are familiar and to a man who is a dear friend to me.

Few of us who were around at the time will ever forget the pain and agony of Watergate. It was a gut-wrenching part of American history and a virtual disaster for the people caught in its web. One of those people was the man who is now my colleague as the executive minister of First Community Church, Jeb Stuart Magruder. At that time, Jeb was a special assistant to President Nixon, directly involved with both the break-in and the cover-up. Consequently, he served seven months in prison.

Today, Jeb rarely talks about the whole mess. Occasionally, he goes out and delivers an address about ethics in a secular society, but to his credit, he does not seek to capitalize on his errors. Rather, he has become a deeper, stronger, more sensitive human being as a result of those difficult days and chooses to let that truth speak for itself.

Still, when he talks about the horror of the experience, he systematically ticks off all of Veninga's points. His first line of recovery came through special friends who stood by him even when the heat was on. Next, he has been forced to make peace with the high price for feeling above the law. As far as guilt is concerned, he has long since acknowledged his mistake and moved beyond it. And finally, through a strong faith and a lot of hard work, he has developed a great reason to live.

Working with Jeb has been an eye-opener for me. He has taught me a great deal about good management. He is a superb administrator and an excellent teacher. But most significant to me, he is a vulnerable, sensitive, solid human being. Our friendship has made me aware of the ruthless dimensions of power, both ways. In the White House, this decent man developed a power-blind indifference to right and wrong. At the same time, when the press sniffed an opportunity to penetrate the invincibility of the presidency, the power-blind shoe changed feet. And, most disturbing to me, those of us on the outside looking in applauded the whole process. Watergate was indeed a tragedy, if for no other reason than the manner in which it exposed the ugly side of the human obsession with power.

So every day, when I walk into my office, I rub shoulders with a guy who has obviously confronted and conquered tragedy. My guess is, most of you do the same. Although your friends may not have endured the extra excruciation of having their problems displayed all over the nation's newspapers, I am sure there are a few who have known the same kind of rejection, condemnation, and despair. What is comforting is to see a guy like Jeb, who has picked up the pieces and proved, through the grace of God, that life can be whole again. He is a child of hope.

7

Hope on the Cutting Edge

TIMELY ISSUES

I would like to enhance this ledger by applying the principles of hope to three of the major issues of our time: peace, power, and terrorism. Each of these presents a formidable challenge to those who would choose hope as a foundation for living. When we possess enough warheads to destroy the world several times over, and our designated leaders make it a monthly habit to exchange accusations and threats, it is hard to be hopeful. When the distance between persons of power and the mass of humanity seems to increase daily, it is hard to be hopeful. And when human beings indiscriminately fire machine guns, plant bombs, and murder innocent people, it is hard to be hopeful.

Yet, to surrender hope would be tantamount to embracing death. I believe we must be hope-filled even in the face of hate. Two thousand years ago a very special person made the same choice. It was not in vain.

A SENSE OF HELPLESSNESS

Some conversations are not intended for children's ears. I must have been less than ten years old when I slipped down the stairs at my grandmother's home and heard such a discourse.

My grandmother lived on U.S. Route 66, just outside Bloomington, Illinois. The highway gave her a livelihood in that she had converted her two-story abode into a "tourist home." It had a neon sign out front reading "Motel," which generated a steady flow of characters, particularly during the summer months. Room and board for a whole family was less than five dollars.

The highway offered other effects as well: the incessant rumble of the big trucks, an uninterrupted supply of dogs and cats, and, occasionally, the terror of an accident. That's what I heard about on the stairs. My uncle was telling the other adults about a horrible crash of a few nights previous. It involved a family car and a truck. The car had burst into flames, and a little boy had been trapped inside. Uncle Gene helped restrain the father, as the child beat on the window, screaming: "Help me, Dad! Help me!" The boy did not survive.

The story made a lasting impression on me—then, as a child imagining what it was like for the boy, and now, as a man, imagining the misery of that father. Either way, what we have here is a consummate definition of helplessness: perceiving disaster, yet being unable to do anything about it.

The proliferation of nuclear weapons and the seeming inability of the superpowers to agree to stop the march toward oblivion prompts an image of all humanity pounding on a window, screaming, "Help us, Lord! Help us!" I know that's tough talk, and variance of opinion regarding the safety of the world at this moment is quite strong. Nonetheless, from the perspective of an American Christian, I would like to pose and respond to the question, How can we choose hope while sitting on a time bomb?

INSIGHT FROM AN EARLIER SIEGE

As a basis for my response to that question, I want to call your attention to the seventh chapter of John, verses 37 through 44. Here we find the Master at the Feast of Tabernacles, addressing a crowd of commoners and Pharisees. The latter are attempting to trap him, the former only to feed on his wisdom.

We need to be aware that the Feast of Tabernacles was a feast of the future. It was the annual celebration of the harvest to come. Occurring in the middle of October, it marked the confidence of the people that God would meet their needs for the winter ahead. It was a symbolic expression of the inner convictions of the Jews, proclaiming, "We believe in tomorrow!"

But Jesus, sensing the preoccupation of the people with material supply, turned their thoughts in a different direction. He said, "If any one thirst, let him come to me and drink. He who believes in me, as the scripture has said, 'Out of his heart shall flow rivers of living water' " (John 7:37-38).

His emphasis is my emphasis. I believe the weakness of the current peace movement and the blindness of the arms race are one and the same. Both are over-concerned with hardware and under-concerned with the nature of humanity. Our hope is not in the manipulation of nuclear weapons systems but in the transformation of the soul of civilization.

If humanity is being betrayed, it is not by the politicians and militarists. They are doing precisely what they have always done: managing governments, preserving systems, and developing means of dominance. The onus of failure lands squarely on those called to proclaim the Word of God. We are the ones who have sold out to the system. Two thousand years ago, God made a clear and concise decision regarding life and death. Ours is the responsibility to center human beings in that decision. Inasmuch as the resurrection of Jesus Christ unequivocally endorses the victory of life over death, and we have so bungled that message that our world is now shrouded with the possibility of total destruction, we have failed miserably.

A VALUES ADJUSTMENT

It is not too late. The button has not been pushed. The trigger has not been pulled. The switch has not been thrown. Like gunfighters on a dusty cow town street, the two superpowers stand face to face, guns drawn, hammers cocked. Now, the battle is for the soul, and that is the domain of the theologian. Nuclear holocaust cannot be avoided through hardware management. It can only be avoided through an inclusive adjustment of the human value system. That starts with you and me.

When I think about the ridiculous proliferation of nuclear weapons systems, I am reminded of *The Life and Times of Judge Roy Bean*. In that motion picture, there is a poignant scene in which the impulsive judge is offended by an itinerant badman. In a wink, the judge draws his six-gun and empties it into his adversary. Then he ceremoniously dons his black robe, summons his clerks, and walks up to the body of the culprit. Pointing, he pronounces the sentence: "Hang him!"

Dead is dead. Blown up is blown up. What difference does it make whether we are blown up once or three hundred times?

THE LOSS OF INNOCENCE

Harold Englund, my predecessor as senior minister of First Community Church, makes it a point to remind us that we have lost our innocence. We have eaten of the nuclear tree of good and evil. We can't pretend there are no nuclear weapons. Now, just like Adam and Eve, our only salvation is in a fresh understanding of our purpose as children of God.

Virginia Mollenkott, the brilliant evangelical theologian, captures the point when she paraphrases the words of Zechariah, "Peace comes not by might, nor by power, but by the Spirit of the Living God" (4:6).

This is the abiding impact of the resurrection. The Romans flexed their might. They grabbed this rabble-rousing preacher and stuck him on a cross. Then they lifted him up for all the world to see. It was an obvious message for anyone who wanted to fiddle with the power of Rome. But they failed to appropriately punctuate the sentence. It was not concluded. To be sure, they didn't have the means to conclude it. And from the silent emptiness of the tomb of Joseph of Arimathea, there thundered a message that outlived the Romans and all their armies, and will outlive the United States and the Soviet Union and Britain and France and any other country so silly as to assume the right to determine the destiny of God's creation.

What is that message? Life is more powerful than death. Love conquers hate. And the Prince of Darkness will one day kneel at the feet of the Prince of Peace.

This is the arena for Christian action. We can stomp

and snort all we want about the stockpiles of weapons, but they will never be neutralized until the will of humanity is centered in the purpose of God.

That's the power of Isaiah's prophecy.

It shall come to pass in the latter days
  that the mountain of the house of the Lord
shall be established as the highest of the mountains,
  and shall be raised above the hills;
. . . .
He shall judge between the nations,
  and shall decide for many peoples;
and they shall beat their swords into plowshares,
  and their spears into pruning hooks;
nation shall not lift up sword against nation,
  neither shall they learn war any more.

(Isaiah 2:2, 4)

The scripture does not say we will be without weapons. It simply says we will choose to do something else with them. Our aim is in error when we direct our concern to missiles, submarines, and spacecraft. We need to be concentrating on the will of humanity. As some wag said, "Bombs don't kill people. People kill people."

QUIETLY EFFECTIVE

Let me take you back to that Feast of Tabernacles and explain a ritual. On the last day a golden pitcher was filled with water from the pool of Siloam. Then, as the people sang, "With joy shall ye draw water out of the wells of salvation," the water was carried up to the Temple where it was solemnly poured into two pipes through which it passed underground into the Kidron Valley.

In this unobtrusive manner the people opened

themselves to the will of God. Water was a precious commodity to them. Their worst memories involved drought, crop failure, and Jerusalem under siege with her water cut off. Hence, they were symbolically vowing to God, "We give of the little we have so as to receive from the plenty which is yours."

I believe the dawn of peace will be born in a similar fashion. Not with a spectacular, datable event, but with the gentle perseverance and faith of a people willing to practice love in order to obtain peace. Like that water trickling under the hustle and bustle of Jerusalem out into the fertile fields of the valley, so the incidental acts of peace offered by men and women of God will trickle under the confusion of political rhetoric, the rattling of sabers, and the positioning of missiles, to the fertile ground of human beings who value life more than death.

Do we want peace? It starts with an intentionally flexible attitude toward those with alien political systems. It continues with the denial of anger and the embrace of understanding. It grows with the way we treat one another, at home, at work, and in the church. It stabilizes with the knowledge that this is a shrinking world and the day fast approaches when we will have no choice but to accommodate new ideas, savor common concerns, and accept the inevitability of coexistence or no existence.

Lewis Thomas crystallizes the issue:

But all in all, looking ahead, it seems to me that the greatest danger lies in the easy assumption by each government that the people in charge of military policy in any adversary government are not genuine human beings. We know ourselves, of course, and take ourselves on faith: Who among us would think of sending off a cluster of missiles to do a million times more damage to a foreign country than was done at Hiroshima, for any reason? None of us, we would affirm. But there are those people on the other side who do not think as we do, we think. (*Late Night Thoughts on Listening to Mahler's Ninth Symphony* [New York: Viking, 1983], p. 9)

I read those words and I could not help but think of the incident recorded by Jimmy Carter in his memoirs. He recalls a special moment in the SALT negotiations when he and Brezhnev, after hassling details all day, found themselves alone ascending a staircase. The Soviet leader reached out, grasped the president's arm, and observed, "If we fail God will never forgive us!"

Later, when Carter publicly shared that remark, Brezhnev was annoyed. He didn't like that image.

What a shame. What a shame that we cannot allow our leaders the privilege of their humanity. I doubt there is a one, here or there, who relishes the thought of a nuclear exchange. And that is our foothold. That is the place where we who know the tune of a different drummer need to seize the advantage. Life is more precious than death.

AN AGENDA FOR LIFE

An appeal for arms control is a matter of material manipulation and ever-awkward verification. Nevertheless, I believe we must make it. On the other hand, an appeal for peace, in the sense in which it is manifested in Jesus Christ, is the highest common denominator of all human beings, a matter of life! Even if we fail at arms control, we must never relax our Christ-centered conviction that life is the most precious of human possessions.

The challenge is not to dehumanize with the threat of destruction but to rehumanize with the promise of peace and the sharing of prosperity. Peace will come not by might, nor by power, but by the Spirit of the Living God.

I believe it was Abraham Heschel who shared the legend about a mythical kingdom faced with the dilemma of having its grain crop poisoned. Every person who ate the grain went insane. Yet if they did not eat, they starved to death. It was a terrible predicament.

Finally, the king called his subjects together. "I have made a very difficult decision. I have decided that we must survive, therefore we will eat the grain. But only on one condition; we will designate a select group to feed on the small uncontaminated food supply. We must have someone around, always, to remind us we are crazy."

On August 6, 1945, in the skies of the Imperial Nation of Japan, the grain crop of civilization was poisoned. Innocence decimated, we began the spiraling race toward Armageddon. But there are still a few citizens practicing a different diet: prayer, hope, love, justice that is oblivious to power , an emphasis on soul reform as a means to social reform, and a vision of peace.

May God grant to these people the means by which to remind others that they are crazy, the courage to proclaim the Word of God, and the strength to choose hope.

It was Dr. Harold Warlick of the Harvard Divinity School who said, "I believe it is profoundly important for some people to live their lives in anticipation of that which the world does not yet have!"

There is not much that we do not have. But something that is increasingly snatched from our grasp is confidence for the future. Well, I don't accept that. To the contrary, I choose to live my life in anticipation of a new heaven and a new earth. I choose to live my life with confidence in God's preference for life and peace.

So let us return to that flaming car adjacent to Route 66. The trapped child screams, "Daddy, help me! Help me!" And what parent would not surrender life to save the boy? Alas, even that was impossible.

Here is the difference.

What the human parent could not do, the Heavenly Parent can.

HOPE AND POWER

In the closing scene of the motion picture *Patton*, we see the fabled general walking past a huge windmill with his faithful dog trotting at his side. As the music signals the end of the film, these words appear across the bottom of the screen: "Sic transit gloria mundi." Translated, they mean "All glory is fleeting." Patton was a man of power, and like so many people of power, his strength seemed to survive for glory. When he was removed from the limelight, he became a sniveling manipulator.

I believe we would not be far from correct if we paraphrased the thought about glory, substituting the word "power": "All power is fleeting."

My mind runs to Bob Greene's revealing interview with Richard Nixon, just a few months ago. The writer asked the former chief executive how he managed to endure all the animosity that has come his way.

"If I had feelings, I probably wouldn't have even survived," he said, "I remember very clearly something. I was speaking down in Williamsburg, Virginia, and this was right after I had become President. And I think we had made the first announcement about our first withdrawal of twenty-five thousand from Viet Nam. And this very pretty girl, she was I guess sixteen, seventeen, came up and spit full in my face and said, 'You murderer.'

"I borrowed a handkerchief from a secret service man and wiped it off, and then I went in and made my speech. It was tough."

In a way, telling that story seemed to bring him to life. It struck me that to anyone else, the key part of the tale would have been the girl's spitting. But Nixon's voice rose and the set of his jaw became firm precisely when he said, "It was tough"; that's what he wanted me to understand—that no matter how badly people treated him, he could not be touched. (*American Beat* [New York: Atheneum, 1983], p. 76)

It is that sense of being untouchable that makes the distance between the people on top and the rest of us seem so huge. We all have a need for some control over our destiny, and although I have made it quite clear that I believe God is ultimately in charge, there is no question but that human beings still maintain the freedom of choice. Choosing hope is only a valid option if people have the power to make the decision. If not, it is a cruel game to place the wonders of hope in front of people who cannot lay claim to it.

So what are the roots of power?

When we examine the roots of power, we need to be reminded that power flashes in a moment but is forged over a period of time. In that memorable passage from Luke where the devil tries to get Jesus to worship him, there is a tell-tale line. The Bible says "The devil . . . showed him all the kingdoms of the world in a moment of time, and said to him, 'If you . . . will worship me, it shall all be yours!' " It was both a gesture of power and a test of power.

But anyone who believes Christ's response was formulated in that instant does not understand power. It doesn't materialize at the snap of a finger. It grows over a period of time, only focused periodically. Real power is rarely displayed. It doesn't have to be. Still, its very presence is a dominant influence.

Choosing hope means recognizing one's right to power, identifying how that power exists, and standing confidently in its strength.

THE ORIGINS OF POWER

John Kenneth Galbraith, former ambassador to India and professor of economics emeritus at Harvard University, carefully examines the issue in *The Anatomy of Power*. According to him, power has three basic sources: (1) personality, (2) wealth, and (3) organization. Any one of these influences can generate power, and where the greatest authority exists, all three are generally present.

I think of three names appearing annually on lists of the world's most respected men: Ronald Reagan, Billy Graham, and Bob Hope. Each is blessed with a unique personality, a solid organization, and an abundance of financial resources. Each is a powerful human being.

Interestingly, all followed different roads in becoming household names in America. Hope capitalized on a quick wit and a compassionate heart, exposed both through radio and motion pictures, then developed an organization that made the most of his gains. Graham built on what I perceive is a genuine faith foundation, an analytical mind, and a gifted oratorical style. And our president used his personality to slip into the world of politics, where he found eager acceptance from an organization in search of a communicator.

For those who see power as a key to the future, it would be wise to examine access to personality, wealth, and organization, as a first step toward choosing hope. It is worth noting that of the three, the only ingredient not readily available to every human being is wealth. And even that one can be overcome if one properly employs the other two. Hope for the oppressed has an exciting way of manifesting itself through superb organization and carefully selected personalities.

But getting power and keeping it are two different issues. Again, Galbraith gives us some insight when he lists the tools of power. He explains the preservation of power as heavily dependent on: (1) punishment, (2) reward, and (3) mind control.

Here, I want to use a negative example to reinforce the theory. Dwell with me on the brief reign of Adolf Hitler. The Führer used personality and organization to secure wealth. Thus empowered, he maintained his muscle through punishment, reward, and mind control. Those who did not cooperate with the Third Reich were destined to barbed wire prisons and gas chambers. At the same time, Hitler's confidants and generals were richly rewarded for their loyalty, being privileged to fancy cars, elegant resorts, an endless succession of women, specially designed uniforms, and seats of respect at all government functions. But the most powerful tool reinforcing Adolf Hitler was one man, Joseph Goebbels. As the minister of propaganda, he shaped the thinking of the German people. Said Goebbels, "If you tell a lie long enough, it becomes the truth." He lied. Hitler led. The world trembled in the balance.

Another rule about power surfaces at this point: Power begets power. Consider the fact that across from Hitler there emerged a Churchill and a Roosevelt. Across from the Axis, there developed the Allies. And in response to the limited wealth of Germany, the combined resources of the free world assured the downfall of the Third Reich.

Now, four decades later, the players have changed but the game remains the same.

The tragic side of power is the manner in which it can smother a person. It takes over. It transforms. And it often destroys. Mother Teresa hit the mark when she said, "The more you have, the less you can give, and the less you have, the more you can give." Sadly, stewardship patterns among Christians confirm her convictions. On a relative basis, people on limited incomes far outgive their more prosperous counterparts.

Lest we lust too deeply for power, let us be reminded that it does have a downside. It seems that as we accumulate the power of wealth, prestige, status, and reputation, we concurrently surrender the gifts of freedom, anonymity, spontaneity, and sacrificial living. Having scrambled to reach the top, people are often blinded by their position.

Observes Søren Kierkegaard: "When it is said, 'Seek ye first the kingdom of God,' . . . it is required above all that man seek not first something else. But what is this 'something else' he seeks? It is the temporal. If then he is to seek first God's Kingdom, he must freely renounce every temporal goal" (*Christian Discourses* [New York: Oxford University Press, 1940], p. 159).

I realize this is a message that will be better received in the tenement houses of New York than in the golden ghettos of America's suburbs. Still, it is a message that liberates in both places.

You see, all human power comes to focus in a single moment. Our hope is only as strong as our confidence in the promise of God as we breathe our last breath. Personality, wealth, and organization to the side, we are all on a limited journey. If Christianity is a farce, then we have cause to feel cheated by the unbalanced distribution of power. But if Christ lives, for us and through us, we are as powerful as any human being who has ever lived.

Said Paul:

> For as by a man came death, by a man has come also the resurrection of the dead. For as in Adam all die, so also in Christ shall all be made alive. But each in his own order: Christ the first fruits, then at his coming those who belong to Christ. Then comes the end, when he delivers the kingdom to God the Father after destroying every rule and every authority and power. For he must reign until he has put all his enemies under his feet. The last enemy to be destroyed is death. (I Corinthians 15:21-26)

If we own that, we own power.

HOPE AND TERRORISM

The Mark of Cowardice

Cockfighting is a savage form of entertainment. Since the days of Themosticles, men have displayed a bent toward barbarism by training gamecocks to do battle, equipping them with two-and-a-half-inch steel spurs, and watching gleefully as they tear each other apart. Although the so-called sport has been outlawed in most parts of the United States, it continues, mostly in the Southwest. A good fighter is worth several thousand dollars. And when two champions get together, hundreds of thousands can change hands at the gambling tables.

The one thing a champion gamecock cannot afford to do is "show the white feather." It constitutes the worst form of cowardice. When one of these ferocious creatures finds himself getting the worst of it and decides to quit, he makes his intent known by lifting his hackles, thereby showing the white feather.

In this light, I feel it would be extremely appropriate to ship a boatload of pale plumage to Beirut, Frankfurt, San Salvador, and, particularly, Libya. During the last few years, the consciousness of the world has been paralyzed by the cowardly acts of terrorists: the vicious murder of Robert Dean Stethem; the hijacking of the *Achille Lauro* with the subsequent death of Leon Klinghoffer; the periodic bombings of airports, nightclubs, and aircraft. All are the deeds of spineless criminals whose hackles are exposed.

In the midst of this, how do we choose hope?

The Goals of Terrorism

We must start with some basic information about terrorism and conclude with some difficult decisions leading to firm action.

Walter Laquer, as chairman of the Research Council of the Center for Strategic and International Studies in Washington, once explained that the primary purpose of all terrorist activity is *publicity*. Life means very little to these people. Exposure, on the other hand, means everything. What they really want is a lot of people watching and a lot of people listening. This is why so much of the resistance movement has left the countryside—where it formerly flourished—and relocated in the cities. Only in metropolitan areas is there ready access to newspaper journalists and television coverage.

Several years ago ABC made the decision to intentionally avoid fan demonstrations when they covered sports events around the world. After years of watching fools charge onto playing fields, disrobe in the stands, and lift up obscene signs, the media people figured out they were being used, that a small minority was wrecking what was a good thing for the greater majority. Now, the ABC directors have been told, "Grant no air-time to ridiculous displays."

Instant Notoriety

A few years ago, a bizarre incident occurred during the "Today" show that firmly underlines this point.

It was graduation day at Columbia University, and Jane Pauley was doing a short spot comparing the student of today with the student of the sixties. Sitting amid a sea of folding chairs set up for commencement, Ms. Pauley was talking with teachers, students, and campus employees. All of a sudden, a young man charged into the picture, tossed a cup of coffee all over her, and fled into an adjacent building.

Like the pro she is, Jane Pauley wiped off her face and continued the interview. The invader was captured, questioned, and released. Several days later, a few of the other students explained that the guy was a third-level figure on campus. He had no identity and had never been in a leadership position. But now, thanks to a disregard for the dignity and human rights of another, he had become a national figure in ten seconds.

No big deal? Right. Speak to me of Oswald, Sirhan, Ray, Brehmer, and Hinkley. Along the same line, take note of where most terrorist activity originates. Publicity has a hypnotic effect on unstable people, and it has an even more hypnotic effect on unstable systems.

Merchants of Fear

In addition to the publicity angle, most terrorist actions have a second goal, which is closely allied to the psychological process of "brain seeding." Agriculturalists tell us that the secret to seeding clouds is not in the immediate response of the cloud to the chemicals but, rather, in the long-range interaction between cirrus clouds and the catalyst. In the same sense, through their utter disregard for life (their own as well as their victims'), terrorists plant seeds in the minds of the free world, forcing a reassessment of values.

That is why so many of us find ourselves poring over information about Islamic sects. We want to understand the concept of *Jihad*, or holy war. We want to understand how life can be so expendable. We want to formulate some rational response to reckless ruthlessness.

But if we are to maintain our hope under the threat of terrorism, we must recognize that rational minds applied to irrational actions come up empty every time. How can a Navy passport justify a bullet in the head? What is the price of the lives of a three-year-old and a five-year-old in a German airport? What is the potential danger in a mother, a daughter, and a granddaughter who have been suddenly sucked through a hole in a jetliner?

These things make no sense at all until we measure their effect on a democratic society. Terrorism doesn't fare too well in totalitarian systems. There seems to be a direct parallel between freedoms granted and lunacies assumed.

Ironically, the record indicates the more injustice and repression in a given country, the less likely the occurrence of terrorist activity. It is not impossible to restrict terrorism in a democratic society, it is just extremely distasteful. Why? Because it calls for stern and unbending postures in a day when flexibility and compromise are hailed as great civil attributes. This is the day of dialogue.

The Right to Be Heard

But shouldn't we consider that the right to dialogue is earned rather than seized? So long as all parties involved are interested in the welfare of the greatest number of people, I feel dialogue is to be applauded. But when dialogue—garnered at the point of a gun—is but a guise for the imposition of minority opinion at the expense of the majority, it is little more than a tool of anarchy.

There is a point where one earns the right to influence the direction of society. There is a point where one earns the right to lead. Minorities do have the right to be heard. That is essential to the preservation of hope. But the domination of the majority due to the financial, political, or terrorist maneuvers of the minority cannot be tolerated. There comes a time when social conscience tells us that people who plant bombs, murder helpless victims, machine-gun public restaurants, and massacre innocent civilians do not have the right to tea, crumpets, and conversation.

Basic Responses

So how do children of hope respond to the threat of terrorism?

First, we express our concern to the American press that they contain their urge to exploit exploitation. Separated from publicity, terrorism fades.

Second, we must affirm our leaders for refusing to engage in dialogue by blackmail and for initiating firm actions in response to terrorist activity.

Third, we must advocate stiff penalties for those

who mock the value of human life by indiscriminately assaulting innocent victims.

And probably most important, we must recognize our calling to confront injustice at every opportunity. Oppression invariably leads to aggression. As choosers of hope, we are obligated to endorse life, assist those who are victims of tyranny, and attack cruelty in every form.

These are trying days. Never before have we possessed the capacity to totally destroy life, and never before have we been surrounded by so many to whom it appears life has no value. It is a time to courageously endorse the future by affirming the uniqueness of all human beings. It is a time to choose hope.

8

Hope in the Midst of Crisis

LIFE WOULD NEVER BE THE SAME

When the alarm sounded at 6:30, the house came alive. Frank headed for the shower, Jane for the kitchen, the kids for their bathroom. After a noisy breakfast, Dad, briefcase in hand, headed for the office. Mom cleared the schedule with Tommy, in his first year of middle school. As he left, she turned to the younger pair. Susan, the fifth grader, appeared bored as Jane knelt in front of Tammy, the kindergartner. "You have a fun day and be sure to thank Mr. Wright for the happy-face note."

At last alone, she poured herself a cup of coffee, picked up the morning paper, and studied Jane Pauley, trying to guess when the baby was due. Twenty minutes later, as she stepped into the shower, the phone rang. She was informed there had been an accident on the playground, and Tammy had been rushed to the hospital. She was told to go to the emergency room at once. The school secretary could tell her nothing more.

Arriving at the hospital, she found Frank waiting.

"What's going on?" she asked. "I don't know, they won't tell me anything," he mumbled.

Just then a young doctor approached. He was painfully precise. "Your daughter has died of head injuries sustained in an accident on the playground this morning. We did all we could. I am very sorry!"

Life would never be the same.

Herb Nelson was a big, quiet man. For ten years he had been scaling steel girders, eating lunch while his feet dangled over the side—sometimes thirty, sometimes forty, sometimes fifty stories high. He was not afraid. He was a pro. He knew what he was doing.

Then, on a Thursday evening, he came home to find a note from his wife. "Herb, I am leaving you. Don't try to find me."

Life would never be the same.

Or what about Morgan Evans, the consummate yuppie? At thirty-seven he was the president of the most prestigious brokerage house in Tulsa, the major stock holder in a new computer firm, and a much sought-after speaker for business conventions all over America. Somehow, all that paled when he was summoned to the office of the high school principal, where he was informed that Morgan Jr. was not only using cocaine but selling it as well.

Life would never be the same.

It happens when the house burns to the ground, or the business collapses, or the marriage disintegrates. It happens when a loved one dies, or illness strikes, or a child disappears. And it happens when the bank says no, or an injury results in paralyzation, or a good friend takes his own life.

A TIME FOR CRISIS

A crisis is a bomb that explodes in the middle of your life and shatters your routine. And crises have no respect for persons. The haunting ditty of the age-old children's game comes to mind:

Ring around the rosie,
Pocketful of posies.
Ashes, ashes,
All fall down.

Sooner or later, no matter who one is, where one lives, how well one plans, or how extensive one's clout, all fall down—crisis strikes. Under such conditions, if we are to choose hope it is to our advantage to know the earmarks of a true crisis, anticipate our behavior, and respond with careful forethought. My goal in this chapter is to set forth a hope-filled approach to dealing with crises.

LEARNING FROM ELAH

For the Israelites, such a moment came in the valley of Elah. Long harassed by the Philistines, Saul finally decided to go to war. He gathered his men and set forth to confront his adversaries. According to the Scripture, the two armies were encamped west of Bethlehem when the crisis came. Suddenly a voice wafted over the valley. "Men of Israel. Let's settle this thing with honor. Send forth one of your men. If he defeats me, you win. But, if I defeat him, we win."

It sounded like a reasonable approach until Saul saw the speaker. Never had he seen a man of such stature. Here was Wilt Chamberlain, André the Giant, and William "Refrigerator" Perry all rolled into one. Historians suggest Goliath was nine and a half feet tall. His armor alone weighed nearly two hundred and fifty pounds. To put it mildly, *he was a surprise*, and neither Saul nor his army knew how to respond. The Bible says, "They were dismayed and greatly afraid."

In this popular Old Testament narrative we will find powerful insight about how to deal with the crises. Dr. Karl Slaikeu, author of one of the most popular textbooks on crisis intervention, explains in *The Phoenix Factor* (Boston: Houghton Mifflin, 1985) that there are three categories of crises.

Interrupted Order

When anything *threatens the established order of our lives*, Slaikeu says that is a crisis. Certainly, when Goliath suggested a "winner take all" showdown, the Israelites were threatened. In like fashion, when one loses a job or is forced to relocate or suffers a crippling injury, the established order of life is threatened, and a crisis is at hand.

I think of the beleaguered Texas oil industry. A few weeks ago, I read an article about the upper level executives who one day commanded corner offices on the upper floors of gleaming office buildings and the next found themselves applying for unemployment compensation. The established order for these guys included yachts on Galveston Bay, multiple memberships in exclusive country clubs, and four-level mansions with five-car garages. Now, insurance companies are taking out full-page ads in the Houston newspapers warning of extensive investigations prior to honoring any fire-loss claims. And still, million dollar suburban homes fall victim to mysterious flames almost every day.

Surprise! Surprise!

A second category of crisis is *any challenge for which one is unprepared*. Any person who has ever heard a physician say, "That's a suspicious mass," knows about this one. Given some lead time, most of us can preserve our dignity in the face of a major hurdle. But when the adversary drops out of the blue, we have a tendency to panic. Sure, I've heard of other people losing their jobs, but not me. Sure, I know that marriages fail all the time, over 50 percent to be exact, but not mine. And, of course cancer has no respect for victims, but it had better respect me.

I think it is a mark of God's grace that most people have a solid core of self-preserving optimism. I occasionally try to imagine what it must have been like to be in the landing craft approaching Omaha Beach. When I see the films of those boats smashing through the waves while explosions crisscross their paths, my gut wrenches with fear. My guess is the majority of those men assumed they would survive, one way or another. They figured there was no bullet bearing their name. Frankly, that's a pretty healthy approach. It saves one from total despair.

But what happens when one gets hit anyway? What happens when the X-rays are suspicious? What happens when a child fails to come home? Or a plane crashes?

Like Saul in the Valley of Elah, we are confronted with a challenge for which we are unprepared. We are caught in a crisis.

In the Wake of Loss

And so we arrive at a third crisis earmark. First, anything that threatens the established order of our lives can be deemed a crisis. Second, anything that presents a challenge for which we are unprepared also qualifies as a crisis. And third, any event constituting *the loss of someone or something important to us* is a crisis.

Here, we think of the obvious: the loss of a spouse, a child, a dear friend—or even the loss of something material, such as a home, a savings account, a family heirloom. Of course, we would be devastated. But think further. Think of the less tangible but equally important impact of losing one's self-esteem, reputation, or pride.

American corporate life is well known for its ladders of success. The most aggressive and astute achievers are always aware of which bases need to be touched, which chairs must be occupied, and which promotions point the way to the top. The best of them also know when they've played out their options. Unfortunately, when I was in seminary they didn't teach us about such networks. Hence, shortly after ordination, I remember my sense of bewilderment over the depression of an earnest young man who had been bypassed at promotion time. I remember talking for hours, trying to convince him it was OK. I kept saying brilliant things like, "Hey, that's a huge company. Your day will come." "Come on, man, perk up! They're saving you for something better."

But he knew the chairs better than I did. He was right. He knew his upward mobility had peaked. His dream had collapsed, and for him, it was crisis time.

I suspect Saul felt the same way when he first gazed at Goliath. Remember, Saul was one tough cookie. He was not accustomed to fear. But then he hadn't encountered too many nine-foot warriors, either. Suddenly, he wasn't the most imposing force in the valley. This guy was big, and ugly, and on the wrong team.

It is worth noting that nearly every crisis we encounter can be tied to a specific event. Sometimes there are a whole lot of things leading up to that event, but just the same, the event touches off the disaster.

Marriages do not collapse in five minutes, but the culminating argument can last less than one. Drug problems rarely evolve overnight, but an overdose can occur in thirty seconds. And most heart attacks take months or years to develop, but the paralyzing pain strikes in an instant. All of which is to underscore the most damaging dimension of any crisis—its explosive emergence. The suddenness stuns and confuses. Consequently, established patterns of behavior evaporate and we feel helpless in the hands of fate.

WHAT HAPPENS WHEN IT HAPPENS

Old methods of coping simply don't work. You take a walk and try to think, but your mind will not clear. You go to a movie seeking intentional distraction, but you may as well be sitting in front of a four-way mirror, every angle reflecting the problem from a different perspective. You try to buy your way to peace but it can't be done; not a new wardrobe, a new car, or even a new house can remove the nagging sense of helplessness created by the crisis.

Next, your emotions go wacko. You are not you anymore. You laugh at things you know are not funny, and you cry at the change of a traffic light. Inside, a whole new parade of feelings develop.

Guilt. You tick off all the private sins through which you have earned this dilemma. If the victim is someone else, you ask, Why isn't this happening to me? And you constantly struggle with the question, What might I have done to prevent this?

Fear. As a cancer patient confided to me, "If it's in my prostate, God knows where else it might be."

Ruth Carlson, whose son was critically injured in a motorcycle accident, just plain couldn't understand her reaction. She wrote:

I think about the accident all the time. I find myself crying sometimes at the strangest times. I feel unsure of myself, more withdrawn.

175

I can't understand these feelings, for I used to be such an optimistic person. I used to get up in the morning full of energy. But now I sleep in, sometimes until ten or eleven o'clock. I don't have the energy to do my work. And I would rather be alone than with my friends.

I don't know what has happened to me. But I just seem unsure of myself. It's kind of like you don't know whether anything is worthwhile any more.

I keep telling myself it is going to get better and it probably will. But right now I sure have lost my confidence. (*A Gift of Hope*, p. 51)

That's how crisis works. It so rattles our routines that we can hardly function, and sitting in the middle of the whole mess is the inevitable question, Why should I continue to live? Depending on the seriousness of the crisis, that question may or may not linger. But it always pops up. It always makes us think.

And that thinking, that reprioritizing, that forced assessment of what makes us run, is the key to conquering the catastrophe.

Jean Paul Sartre said it: "You cannot understand being [life] until you comprehend non-being [death]."

So there you have it, an analysis of a crisis. And if you are unable to identify with what you are reading, let me assure you, one day you will. One day you will camp in the Valley of Elah. One day you will stand in the shadow of Goliath.

When it happens, what will you do?

THE LINGERING EFFECT OF CRISIS

The television cameras were long gone; the waves were still there. The helicopters no longer thumped their muffled alarms; the waves were still there. And the palm trees ceased their genuflections before the now departed eighty-mile-per-hour winds, but the waves were still there.

It had been four days since the eye of Hurricane Camille passed through Biloxi, and though it was no longer front-page news, the sea was yet to forget. Hour after hour, day after day, the angry waves gathered energy and slammed into the beach. Those who live near the sea will tell you that's the way it is with a big storm. Long after the initial turmoil, the ocean continues to churn.

People are the same way. Besieged by trauma, it takes a long time for us to settle down. Some never do.

After all, surviving a crisis does not depend on a big bank account, a stadium full of friends, or a highly polished, psychologically adept vocabulary. Surviving a crisis depends on the choices we make and what we do along the way.

MANAGING PAINFUL FEELINGS

The first consequence of any crisis is a megadose of overwhelming feelings. Can you imagine how Saul must have felt the first time he saw Goliath? Several words come to mind: stunned, petrified, challenged, trapped, doomed.

Or try to identify with a young mother as she is informed that her five-year-old has been killed. The stomach knots, the brain freezes, and the soul goes blank. Then come the angry waves: helplessness, denial, frustration, anger, hate, and maybe even thoughts of self-destruction.

Years ago I came across a phrase used by the therapist Jack Gibb. He said, "Any unexpressed feeling is a potentially sick feeling." In other words, if we don't choose how to get those feelings out, they will take their own route, and it's usually destructive.

177

I will never forget the time my dad left a can of aerosol spray in the back window of the family car while he was playing golf. The sun pounded on the window for a couple of hours and then the can detonated, shattering the window and slicing a hole in the steel roof of the car. The force was unimaginable.

It's the same way with unexpressed feelings born in the midst of crisis. They fester and boil until they explode, adding damage to damage, doing nothing to reduce the problem.

So the first challenge in managing painful feelings is accepting the feeling for what it is. Believe it or not, it's OK to be angry, it's OK to be depressed, and it's OK to feel sick to your stomach. What's not OK is to pretend such passions are not present when all the while they are boiling inside.

One of the best ways to handle such feelings is to see them as Geiger counters from past experiences. The truth is, most passions are hinged to previous events. Hence, when you have been paralyzed by painful feelings, a good first step is to consciously complete the following sentence: "The last time I felt like this was . . ."

You'll be amazed at the perspective this brings. Had Saul done this he might have recalled that knot that developed in his stomach when he led his armies against Amalek. At the same time, he would have noted God's deliverance of those fierce fighters into his hands.

In remembering the past we are frequently empowered in the present. We are also reminded of unfinished business from yesterday that may well be shaping today. In short, we are making contact with reality. And reality is the foundation from which all feelings must be managed.

PRACTICING HEALTHY EXPRESSION

If the first step in managing painful feelings is a matter of identification and acceptance, the second calls us to hit the pressure valve and practice healthy expression.

Here I want to be very careful. In my opinion, one of the most destructive contributions of the "Me Generation" has been the idea that confrontation is our only means of expression. Under that illusion, all these painful feelings I've been talking about will have to be dumped on somebody else. While that might be helpful in some cases, I simply do not believe it's a good rule of thumb.

So what are some options?

One of the most creative approaches to expressing feelings is what I call the "Mythical Madison Square Garden Method." Having identified your feelings, you imagine yourself standing in the center of Madison Square Garden. The stands are filled with every person who you think needs to know your feelings. Maybe it's the president of the United States or your father who has been dead for twenty years or your estranged and unapproachable spouse. They are all equipped with notepads and writing instruments, sworn to silence, and guaranteed to listen. So let'em have it. Make your speech, state your case, dump those feelings.

Of course, the place to do this is in the privacy of your office, or while walking in an open field, or alone in your automobile.

Oh yes, if you really want maximum benefit from this exercise, I suggest two supplemental ideas. When you make that imaginary guest list, be sure to invite people on both sides of the issue. You might even write out the list. And second, try to deliver your address beyond the eyes and ears of others. Innocent passers by and walk-on family members probably won't understand.

Now, if you're not very good at oratory, another wonderful way to express painful feelings is to write them out. Just sit down and record what you feel bubbling inside. Don't hold back. Remember all the while that YOU are in charge of what is done with the final document. Maybe you'll put it in a time capsule, or hide it in the family Bible, or just burn it up. It doesn't matter. What matters is that you identify and express your feelings.

And, by the way, there are two rather common developments at this point, which I want to encourage you not to avoid. First, if you feel like crying, do it. God didn't give us tear ducts solely for the purpose of washing our eyeballs. Slaikeu tells us, "Tears play a direct role in alleviating stress by releasing two important chemicals—leucine-enkephalin and prolactin—which are thought to be part of the body's supply of natural pain-relieving substances called endorphins" (*The Phoenix Factor*, p. 10).

And, second, don't hesitate for a moment to blame God for your predicament.

There is virtually no doubt in my mind regarding Saul's first prayer after spotting Goliath: "Hey, Good Buddy, what in the heck are you trying to do to me?" It's a fair question.

I recall the words of an itinerant preacher I heard in the late sixties. "God can take all the anger we've got and give us love in return. If he answered Golgotha with Easter, what makes us think our temper tantrums will stunt his affection?"

You know, there is no such thing as a right or wrong feeling. There are only real feelings. Sure, they are almost always a matter of perception, and sometimes perceptions are erroneous. But until we come to terms with what we think is true, we are unable to overcome any crisis.

When Saul gazed at Goliath he saw an insurmountable problem. He couldn't imagine how to conquer this big, mean fighting machine. And it wouldn't go away. The Bible says, "For forty days the Philistine came forward and took his stand, morning and evening."

And that prompts yet another observation. If it is helpful to accept and express our feelings, it is even more helpful to control them.

This doesn't mean we bury them. It just means we defuse their dominance.

A Time to Laugh

One of the best ways to do this is through laughter. Sure, there are some crises that are simply too painful to laugh about. But there are very few so devastating as to stunt laughter within. Even as tears liberate healing endorphins into our systems, so does laughter—in fact, more so.

I remember calling on an old friend just a few hours before he went into open-heart surgery. He was a crusty old rascal who was scared to death. Still, with a twinkle in his eye, he said: "Barry, I got it figured out. When they get in there, they're gonna find out I'm runnin' on Jack Daniel's and creosote and nothin' can stop me." I hugged him as we laughed.

Likewise, I will never forget the forty-seven-year-old woman facing a second radical mastectomy who confided in me, "I can't wait to get out of here and go shopping. It'll be the first time in my life I ever bought anything but a 32-A."

Henry Ward Beecher said it:

Mirth is God's medicine. Everybody ought to bathe in it. Grim care, moroseness, anxiety—all this rust of life ought to be scoured off by the oil of mirth. It is better than emery. Every man ought to rub himself with it. A man without mirth is like a wagon without springs, in which everyone is caused disagreeably to jolt by every pebble over which it runs.

Crises are not pebbles, but they can often be put in perspective by a good laugh.

A Time to Wait

A second method of controlling painful feelings is what I call "shelving it." I got this one from Leslie Weatherhead. As he dealt with the horrors of German bombing raids in World War II London, he regularly encountered issues without answers, emotional mazes from which there appeared to be no exit. After months of sleepless nights, he labeled the second drawer on the right side of his desk "Awaiting Further Light." Thereafter, whenever he ran into an unmanageable issue, he would write it on a slip of paper and put it in the "Awaiting Further Light" drawer. Mind you, he wasn't denying the existence of the problem, he was just taking control of it.

We can do the same thing with our feelings. Once we have identified and expressed them, it is to our distinct advantage to take command of them.

A COLLISION OF PICTURES

"We hold these truths to be self-evident, that all people are created equal, that they are endowed by their Creator with certain unalienable rights, that among these are life, liberty, the pursuit of happiness, and steadily ascending careers, fiftieth wedding anniversaries, and eighty-fifth birthdays."

We all know our forefathers didn't write it that way, but nonetheless, that's the way most of us perceive our privileges.

In his book *How to Take Effective Control of Your Life,* William Glasser suggests that our minds function like mammoth picture albums. As the years pass, the albums grow, as we store every experience. For example, let me share some concepts and let's just see what kind of images pop into our minds: supermarket, stallion, coach, doctor, love, politician, vacation. You see, for every concept there is a corresponding picture already situated in our heads. That's just the way human beings function. Crises occur when the pictures in our minds collide with the presence of reality—when the "coach" doesn't talk softly and smoke cigars, or the "doctor" doesn't touch your hand when she talks to you, or the "supermarket" isn't bright and airy and permeated with elevator music.

Put yourself in Saul's sandals for a moment and imagine what kind of pictures he carried. I suspect there was one for a good soldier, another for the experience of battle, and still another for an enemy warrior. But I am quite certain there was nothing to match Goliath. When the Israelite king leaned around his tent to see which Philistine was issuing these crazy challenges, his Kodak Carousel had to jam.

That's what happens when expectations and reality fail to coincide. So let me return to those previously mentioned "unalienable rights." Steadily ascending careers? For some that's a reality, for most it is not! Fiftieth wedding anniversaries? For some that's a reality, for most it is not! And what about eighty-fifth birthdays? Only a few get to blow out eighty candles. In other words, in the three areas psychotherapists note as most loaded with expectations, most of us are going to experience picture-crushing disappointments. Our careers will not be meteoric. Our marriages will not lead to mated beach chairs on Sanibel Island. And the length of our lives will be cut short by unforeseen problems.

In short, our idyllic pictures, patterned in our youth, programmed by parents and other role models, and prescribed by the environment through which we have grown, are destined to fade in the pounding sun of reality. When it happens, the only way to survive is to change pictures, the only way to weather the storm is to change our minds. And that's the next step in coping with crisis.

INTENTIONALLY CHANGING THE MIND

Of course, some folk never get around to this. Refusing to recognize the distortion of their original pictures, they cling to them in defiance of reality. You know people like that, and so do I. They spend a lot of time talking about yesterday, totally oblivious to today. Theirs is a world of distant memories, immediate grief, and long-range loneliness. Unable to change their minds, they seem helpless in the hands of fate. It is as if they ran out of film, can't create new pictures, and will not accept the truth of the moment.

In short, they simply refuse to be honest with themselves.

A close look at the record would lead us to believe that is exactly how Saul was dealing with Goliath. Unable to comprehend how to defeat the huge Philistine, Israel's best simply pretended he was not there. It's a common ploy when crisis strikes. Unfortunately, it does not work.

So the enemy has a nine-foot fighting machine—denying his existence won't make him go away. So the marriage is over—denying it is finished does nothing for the future. So you've reached the pinnacle of your career—hiding from that truth will not change your position.

ACCEPTING THE TRUTH

If we would change our minds and adjust our pictures to deal with reality, we must begin by accepting the truth. Nobody wants to dwell in the Valley of Elah, but only a fool denies arrival. Likewise, few of us look forward to the shadow of Goliath, but when the darkness falls it is prudent to call it for what it is.

Years ago, I shared such a moment with a fragile young mother, as she fingered the sundress of her departed three-year-old daughter. "Hillary is gone," she said; "no matter what I do, I can't bring her back, so I have to give myself to Dick and Matthew." It was a turning point, a time of letting go. I remember putting my arm around her, feeling the warmth of her tears on my shoulder, and inwardly applauding her courage in that moment.

Those who survive tragedies will tell you that's an unavoidable intersection. Choosing hope means there simply comes a time when the painful truth must be acknowledged in order to open the door to the future.

So bare-faced honesty is the first move in changing our minds. Another comes when we define the meaning of the moment.

THE MEANING OF THE MOMENT

What does the crisis mean for the past, for the present, and for the future?

Those of you who own a personal computer are aware of the mind-boggling array of software programs available to help us process words, balance bank accounts, manage projects, and even coordinate our love lives. And for each program there is usually a clone, similar but slightly different. In each case, the program defines expectations and sets the limits on what we can and cannot do.

Well, people are not terribly unlike computers in this respect; we are all running on different programs. Although there are a lot of similarities, no two of us have exactly the same pictures. Hence when crisis strikes, we would do well to reshape our expectations. The goal in changing our minds is not to leap into the abyss of failure. It is to reckon with reality and grow through the valley. It is to admit that some programs fail the test of time. It is to confront the truth, consider its meaning, and count unconditionally on the grace of God.

DISTORTED EXPECTATIONS

Back in 1977, a couple of doctors from Illinois wrote a paper about distorted expectations. Talk about programs that fail the test of time—these concepts are extremely destructive. They are also painfully common.

1. I am a helpless, innocent victim. Unhappiness and what occurs in life are caused by outside circumstances or past events for which I am not responsible and have no control.
2. My worth is measured by my performance.
3. Other people are happy, "normal," and do not have feelings or problems similar to mine. In fact, some people have perfect marriages, perfect children, and ideal jobs.

4. I should retaliate and get even with the world.
5. I should always be calm, cool, and collected and never lose control.
(D. C. Hammond and K. Stanfield, *Multi-dimensonal Psychotherapy: A Counselor's Guide for the MAP Form* [Champaign, Ill.: Institute for Personality and Ability Testing, 1977])

All of these are distorted, unfair expectations that must be confronted and corrected if we are to overcome the crises in our lives. The truth is, we can never deal with trauma if we refuse to confess our humanity and face the fact that our ultimate strength is from the Lord. This is the premier prerogative in choosing hope.

THE SIMPLE TRUTH

In contrast to those distorted expectations, feed on the following insights from another book, a little older and much better read.

If you feel like a *victim*, recall Paul's words to Timothy:

If we have died with him, we shall also live with him;
if we endure, we shall also reign with him;
if we deny him, he also will deny us;
if we are faithless, he remains faithful—
for he cannot deny himself.

(II Timothy 2:11-13)

If you feel unworthy of God's love and understanding, consider again the words of our Lord:

Are not two sparrows sold for a penny? And not one of them hairs of your head are all numbered. Fear not, therefore; you are of more value than many sparrows. (Matthew 10:29-31)

And if you are trapped in a struggle for perfection, pause to reflect on the words of the psalmist:

For who is God, but the Lord?
  And who is a rock, except our God?—
It is God alone who girded me with strength
  and makes my way safe.

(Psalm 18:31-32)

If the first part of changing our minds is facing the truth, the second is identifying our distorted expectations. No marriage lasts forever. No career is without flaw. And no life exceeds by a single second the loving plan of God.

NOT CONFORMED BUT TRANSFORMED

And that brings us to a key thought about mind-changing in the midst of crises. In the twelfth chapter of Romans, we find Paul writing to a bunch of people trapped between the proverbial rock and hard place. On the one side they were thrilled with the promises of Christ and the working of the Spirit in their midst. On the other they were petrified by the might of Rome and the obvious displeasure of the emperor with anything smacking of the Christian faith. They were under tremendous pressure to abandon their beliefs and claim the glittering power of Caesar.

To this, Paul said:

I appeal to you therefore, brethren, by the mercies of God, to present your bodies as a living sacrifice, holy and acceptable to God, which is your spiritual worship. Do not be conformed to this world, but be transformed by the renewal of your mind, that you may prove what is the will of God, what is good and acceptable and perfect. (Romans 12:1-2)

When besieged by crisis, there is no counsel more prudent than that. When the doctor's diagnosis is damning, the judge's gavel renders the marriage dead, the kid you trained becomes your boss, or tenure is denied, dwell on the power of Paul's counsel. Although the outside might change, the inside belongs to God, who is good, and acceptable, and perfect. Viktor Frankl made this discovery in the filthy barracks of a Nazi concentration camp. As he witnessed the deaths of thousands, noted his own physical emaciation, and stared in horror at the wisping smoke of the roaring ovens, he recognized that the gap between what happens TO us and what happens IN us is virtually non-negotiable without personal consent. They could do whatever they wanted to do TO him. But no matter what they did, they could not destroy his FAITH.

THE POWER TO BELIEVE

Hence, we encounter our greatest asset in changing our minds. No matter the challenge, ours is the choice to place it in the hands of the Master and grow through it all.

Often, crises do us a tremendous favor by forcing us to deal with our distorted expectations. They compel us to replace shattered pictures with new ones based on balance and reality. They make us recognize our need for the grace of God.

So picture with me the scene when David kicked open the flap on his brother's tent. My guess is they were glad to see him and more so to see his care package from home. As he tossed out the chocolate chip cookies, opened the M&Ms, and popped the top on the cherry cola, they were probably laughing and hugging, jiving and teasing, as brothers always do. And then Goliath made his speech.

"Whoa, what was that?" asked David. Now remember, this was a kid who fought lions and tigers for kicks. His brothers, veterans of Goliath's jibes, didn't even acknowledge the question. They were chowing down.

"Hold it!" David shouted.

"Who is that guy?"

Now, they probably stopped and stared at him. "Forget it, little brother. This is big-time stuff. You don't want to get involved."

"Didn't he taunt the might of Israel?"

"Yes."

"Didn't he belittle your courage and manhood?"

"Sort of."

"And didn't he suggest you were all a bunch of sissies, unworthy of the name 'warrior'?"

And his oldest brother suggested that David go back and manage the sheep and leave the fighting to the men.

But the boy refused to conform to the pattern set by his brothers. To the contrary, he demonstrated what happens when we are transformed by an inner faith. He said, "Who is this clown who would defy the armies of the living GOD?" And with that, he set forth to see the king and secure permission to engage Goliath.

When we find ourselves in the Valley of Elah, we need to remember that scene.

What role are you playing? Are you Saul, surprised, confused, and feeling abandoned? Or are you like the brothers of David, pretending there is no problem, waiting for someone else to relieve the pressure? Or are you David, on the outside woefully inadequate to cope with the problem, but on the inside loaded with the conviction that

He will raise you up on eagle's wings,
Bear you on the breath of dawn,
Make you to shine like the sun,
And hold you in the palm of his hand.

("On Eagle's Wings")

SPOTTING THE OPPORTUNITY

Long before our modern harbors, sailors would find themselves sitting outside the port waiting for the flood tide, to be certain it was safe to proceed to shore. The term for this situation in Latin was *ob portu*, that is, a ship standing over against a port, waiting for the precise moment to move. Our word "opportunity" issues from this origin.

Even so, I would observe that a person in crisis is a person *ob portu*, a person poised on the brink of opportunity. Seizing that opportunity is but a matter of moving in the right direction.

As Saul sat pondering the insurmountable threat of Goliath, he had no idea what God was doing behind the scenes. Based on the resources at hand, the Israelites were in big trouble. But who ever said we are limited to the resources at hand? Even as Saul was wringing his hands, scratching his head, and pacing his tent, God was at work swelling the tide. David was on his way. To be sure, the Creator was preparing to open a whole new era in Israelite history.

My conviction is that the Master does the same thing in the midst of our crises. Our challenge is to be prepared to seize the moment and change directions. Now, there are several steps in that process.

For starters, we must open our options. I am convinced that for too many of us, our God is simply too small.

Again, we learn from the scene at Elah. David has

191

finally convinced Saul that he can fight Goliath. Impetuously, the great king gestures toward his armor, "Put it on, kid, you're my man!" So David clanks, cranks, squiggles, and squirms until he is inside the armor. Now, he's got a problem. He can't move! The steel weighs more than he does. And for an instant it appears the whole program must be scrapped. Saul starts wringing his hands, scratching his head, and pacing again until out of the corner of his eye he spots the shepherd boy's hand dangling something for him to see. Turning his head, he opens his options and sees the sling.

Nothing Has Always Been This Way

One of the most important dimensions of seizing the moment in the midst of a crisis is the call to break the bonds of history. The old phrase, "It's always been this way," is a lie. Nothing has "always been this way," and the more intentionally we pursue new insights the more effectively we will seize God's grace.

I delight in the story so often related by Harry Emerson Fosdick about the missionary John Paton. It seems Paton once visited the New Hebrides Islands during an extended drought. The natives were observing all kinds of rituals, seeking to coax rain from the sky. At last, the missionary gave them a single command: "Dig!" The natives couldn't believe it. They stared back and forth at each other. "What did you say?" "I said 'Dig!'" "But," they contested, "water comes from the sky." The missionary persisted and the natives complied. Of course, they found the water for which they were searching.

Besieged by crisis, seeking to choose hope in the face of despair, we are all well advised to unshackle our images of God and let the Creator work. Believe it or not, a God of love can bring a blessing through a broken marriage, a lost job, and even a terminal illness.

The Faith-filled Friend

Please note that although Saul had the problem, David's faith answered it. The king was imprisoned by precedents, the kid was empowered by God's promises. That's the value of a faith-filled friend.

Robert Louis Stevenson once observed, "A friend is a present you give yourself." I believe that truth is magnified tenfold when that friend is filled with faith. And for heaven's sake, let's be clear that being filled with faith and being filled with answers are two different things. Very few of us covet advice and directions when we're groping for strength. At the same time, rare is the person who does not take energy, vigor, and comfort from the gentle presence of one who believes and trusts.

There is no substitute for a friend, and a faith-filled friend is simply irreplaceable.

Analytical Intelligence

Now, a third step in seizing the moment in the midst of crisis involves using your whole head!

Current research indicates both the left brain and the right brain play major roles in dealing with a crisis.

Paul Tillich once observed, "The first duty of love is to listen." During the last few years we've heard a lot about listening. In fact, it might be listed as the number one rage in character assessment. Well, when crisis strikes, it is a good idea to listen, especially to yourself. That's a left-brain activity. It calls for the wisdom to weigh the words we find ourselves using all the time. If we're spouting terms like "devastated," or "broken," or "rotten," or "jerk," or "witch," our chances of seizing the moment are extremely slim. Caught up in anger and pain, we need to cross the line of blaming and naming and begin the process of knowing and growing. When that happens we'll find ourselves using words like, "challenged," or "learning," or "encouraged," or "blessed."

Now, at the same time that the left brain is listening and analyzing, the right brain helps us seize the moment by picturing God's promises fulfilled. "Yea, though I walk through the valley of the shadow of death, I will fear no evil. . . . Thy rod and thy staff, they comfort me" (Psalm 23:4 KJV).

One could modify that familiar old psalm and really put it in perspective: "Yea, though I walk through the valley of" the loss of a child, the end of a marriage, the challenge of disease, the collapse of a career,—it doesn't matter, picturing God's promise fulfilled will generate peace and courage we never knew we had.

Just note the image David set before Saul. "Look, man, I have slipped into the night to choke a lion. I have dropped out of a tree to slay a bear. If God protected me there, why should I sweat the bad-breathed brute on the other side of the valley?"

There is a picture that frequently pops into my mind when I am caught in life's whitewater. It comes from the very last chapter of Matthew, when the Lord is leaving the disciples. It's a sad scene. They've really shared the journey and now he is saying good-bye. I suspect there were many heads hanging and no shortage of tears. Spotting this, Jesus consoled them with words suggesting both action and imagery.

All authority in heaven and on earth has been given to me. Go therefore and make disciples of all nations, baptizing them in the name of the Father and of the Son and of the Holy Spirit, teaching them to observe all that I have commanded you; and lo, I am with you always, to the close of the age. (Matthew 28:18-20)

And so we arrive at the fourth step in seizing the moment. First, we open our options. Second, we find a faith-filled friend. Third, we use our whole heads. And fourth, we claim some control.

The Right to Choose

No matter how difficult the crisis might be, a moment of intentional reflection will highlight some area completely under our control. It may be as simple as saying, "I will not call that person again." Or choosing which doctor will perform the surgery. Or picking up another three-year-old and giving her a hug.

What matters is not the magnitude of the action but the meaning of making a choice.

For David the moment came when he dumped the armor. Sure, he could have satisfied Saul and clunked out to meet Goliath, but he wouldn't have been able to lift his arm, let alone swing his sling.

I think of the Type A executive living in the suburbs of Chicago. Every night he would stagger red-faced and enraged into the kitchen, having battled the bumper-to-bumper chaos of the Kennedy Expressway. As his blood pressure continued to rise and the medicinal martinis multiplied, it was obvious he had to do something to address the problem. One day, during the coffee hour after church, he laughingly described his problem to one of the counseling ministers. "Why don't you take control?" said the listener. The executive looked at him incredulously, certain the preacher was a naïve idiot who had never known the agony of rush-hour traffic. "Oh no," responded the minister, properly interpreting the look. "I don't mean control of the whole expressway. I just mean your portion of the road. You can load up with good cassette tapes, maybe even learn a new language, and every now and then, just to show some authority, intentionally let somebody cut in front of you." That harried executive now speaks French and Italian and sees himself as the Robin Hood of the Kennedy forest.

And so we arrive at the final step in choosing hope in the midst of crisis. After we have opened our options, found our faith-filled friends, used our heads, and claimed a corner of control, we conclude by pinpointing the pearl.

The Treasure Within

Long ago, a sage observer noted, "For everything there is a season, and a time for every matter under heaven." In other words, nothing happens for nothing. If we are willing to search, we can find something valuable in every life event. Not always clear in the instant, time has a way of often revealing treasure buried in the worst of traumas.

A Greek philosopher put it this way: "It is not good for all our wishes to be filled; through sickness we recognize the value of health; through evil, the value of good; through hunger, the value of food; through exertion, the value of rest."

I know that may sound terribly naïve in the shadow of a terminal illness or when we are amid the vacuum left by a lost loved one. But please, put it in a broader perspective. Our Lord has promised a peace that passeth all understanding to those who trust in him. We can't explain life before or beyond the points of conception and death. We also can't explain the resurrection. Nevertheless, the Bible clearly states the love of God exceeds both those boundaries. Trusting, we are free to pinpoint the pearl in every crisis.

When Joni Eareckson snapped her neck in a diving accident at nineteen, it was a terrible tragedy. It didn't seem fair. Yet today, Joni would tell you the accident was her gateway to a witness for Christ that has spanned the globe and continues to change lives wherever she goes. What for many might have been an insurmountable burden has for Joni become a bandwagon for the love of God. Sure, it took some adjustment, but she pinpointed the pearl.

That's a process that is open to all of us when we are confronted with crisis. We can wallow in the horror of it all, or we can trust the ultimate grace of God and set out to find the deeper meaning of the experience. We can practice futility or choose hope.

Marilee Zdenek put it this way:

Being at one with the total self,
Accepting all that has been and will be,
Knowing that pain is not alien to joy
But the dark thread enriching the pale tapestry.
. . . .
It isn't easy.*

We all know she is right. We also know the pressure of being *ob portu*, trapped in trauma yet poised on the brink of opportunity.

It's a frightening place to be alone.

It's a wonderful place to be with him.

THE ACTION OPTION

The wind-chill factor was thirty-seven degrees below zero as Dr. Robert Veninga trudged across the campus of the University of Minnesota. Staring at his

---

*Marilee Zdenek, *Splinters in My Pride* (Waco, Tx.: Word, 1979), p. 38

feet squeaking through the winter snow, he thought about the classes yet to be taught and the committee meetings to follow. It wasn't a great day. In fact, it was a bummer—too many classes, too many students, too many responsibilities, and too many committees. He could feel his brain shifting into low gear to accommodate the load.

Then, for some reason, he looked up. In front of him was the Masonic Cancer Center, and up there on the fourth floor, the place where only the most acute cases were handled, he spotted a huge, hand-lettered sign. "I need a large double-cheese and sausage pizza!" Dr. Veninga laughed out loud. Later, a nurse explained to him that by noon that patient's room was filled with pizzas. They had enough to feed everyone on the unit. Veninga relates that story in his timely book *The Gift of Hope*, which has been invaluable to me in my research.

To be sure, I want to lift up that sign maker as a role model for all of us who might fold when crisis strikes. Caught in the deluge of misfortune, the choice of *doing something* to lighten the burden is a stroke of genius. In short, if we would conquer our crises, we must resort to action.

I'm not so silly as to assume the pizza cured the cancer. I am so sensitive as to be certain it changed that day, and conquering crisis is a day-by-day challenge. In that sense, action is the issue. When we study the action potential of the human being, we come up with four areas where activity can be measured.

First, we have *doing* behavior, that is, voluntary actions which are almost entirely under the control of the individual.

Second, we have *thinking* behavior. This is the theater of the mind, where the individual has majority control, with the notable exception of dreams.

Third, there is *feeling* behavior. Our control is

198

considerably reduced in this area, since feelings are largely reactions to external developments.

And finally, we have *physiological* behavior, involving bodily responses over which we have almost no control whatsoever; we get sweaty palms when the pressure mounts, or red blotches as our nervous system goes on alert, or dilated eyes as fear sets in.

DOING DOES THE TRICK

Now, all four of these behavioral categories are important when confronted by crises, but none more so than the first. Whereas we have relatively minor control over what we think, feel, and physically experience, we have almost total control over what we do in a given situation. Thus, the best way to manage our feelings, thoughts, and experiences is through intentional choices about what we do.

So let's go back to the Valley of Elah for the big showdown. Muse with me about what David must have been feeling, thinking, and experiencing as he left Saul's tent. I am sure he was filled with fear, bewildered by thoughts of the odds against him, undoubtedly sweating like a post-Derby thoroughbred. Nevertheless, he chose to walk on. He chose to shake off the taunts of his adversary. He chose which stone to put in his sling. And he chose when to fire his shot.

When we are confronted by a crisis, we cope with attitude, but we conquer with action!

No matter how well we have analyzed the situation, no matter how many positive thoughts we have mainlined to our brains, and no matter how carefully we have reconstructed our values, there comes a time for action, a time to do something.

And we cannot err if our first action is prayer.

A Priority on Prayer

Isn't it fascinating how, face to face with the most fearsome warrior the Hebrews had ever known, David placed his confidence in the hands of God? "You come to me with a sword, but I come to you in the name of the Lord of hosts, the God of the armies of Israel" (I Samuel 17:45 RSV).

A great first step in adjusting our behavior in response to a crisis is the private practice of prayer.

I think of the thirty-three-year-old nurse who went through a painful divorce. She wrote:

Our marriage was not made in heaven, but we did have some pretty good moments together. Andy was no villain. He was hurting as much as I was over our impending divorce. Nevertheless, we both knew that we would be better off not living with one another.

I'll never forget the night Andy packed his bags and left the house. He kissed me at the door and, fighting back tears, thanked me for the good times we had.

That night I could not sleep. I felt totally abandoned. I feared that I would be alone for the rest of my life. I cried and, without even thinking, prayed, "God, please—don't you abandon me too!"

Day after day I struggled with my loneliness. One night I knelt by my bed just like I did as a kid. I just said, "God, if you can hear this, please help me."

That night I fell asleep right away and for the first time in months slept soundly. But in the morning all the terrible fears came back. But I prayed again and asked God to help me through this mess.

I have been saying little prayers now for over five months. I have some terribly difficult days. But I am starting to have some good ones too. I feel stronger. I feel that maybe I can put together the fractured parts of my life. (Veninga, *A Gift of Hope*, p. 215)

You see, prayer is a marvelous *doing* activity. It is a conscious action enveloping every dimension of life with the power of God. It may not result in on-the-spot fireworks and consequences, but it never fails to shape the future and sensitize the pray-er to the unfailing love of the pray-ee.

To that end, I want to suggest a format for prayer during days of crisis. In an effort to manage feelings, cope with questions, search for security, and reach for courage, I'd like to propose that each of the following incomplete sentences be incorporated into our prayers. It might even be a good idea to jot them down on a three-by-five-inch card and keep them in your Bible.

1. Dear Lord, today I feel . . .
2. Master, what I need most from you today is . . .
3. God, today I want to give you . . .
4. Lord, let me ask . . .

Experience has taught me such an approach generates a marvelous sense of perspective and an inner spiritual peace. There is simply no substitute for direct communication with God. Even if we're doing nothing but dumping our anger, talking to the Lord is the best behavioral adjustment we can ever make. Frankly, I find it hard to believe one can truly choose hope without practicing prayer.

Priming and Timing

A second alternative has to do with the way we manage ourselves personally. Virtually every book I have read about managing crisis underscores the necessity of taking care of one's physical self when the pressure is peaking. Some kind of physical exercise is a must, even if it's just a matter of walking around the block every night before going to bed.

Also, sleep is considered a prime asset in confronting

crisis. It may sound silly, but the old adage, "Sleep on it!" is superb counsel. Of course, we all know that as anxiety increases sleep has a tendency to decrease, and we get caught in a vicious circle any time we try to force sleep. All of us who have stared wide-eyed at a 3:00 A.M. ceiling know that. And that's where the "yellow pad" comes into the picture. One of the healthiest pieces of advice I have ever received came from an older minister who once suggested that I keep a yellow pad and a Flair pen on the nightstand next to the bed. "Unfinished business is usually what keeps us awake," he said. "Just write down the issues and ideas on the pad and trust yourself to address them in the morning."

It was good advice, and it leads me to still another dimension of personal management during crisis. Yes, we must be physically attentive during the trauma. We also need to plan for peak-period performance. All of us have certain periods of the day when we are at our best. Some people are "morning people," some "afternooners," and others "all-nighters." Most of us know our most productive time zones. For me, it's the first three hours of the day. That's when I do all my sermon preparation and the majority of my administrative planning. I have learned that this is the time when my mind is most alert and my creative juices really flow. On the other hand, I have learned to stifle the urge to write or design in the evening. If I don't, I usually end up rewriting in the morning.

Hence, when we are caught in a crisis, it is extremely prudent to plan to address the difficult issues during our peak-performance periods.

Best estimates place the final conflict between David and Goliath at midday. My guess is that was a perfect fit for David. Accustomed to rising with the dawn to tend his sheep, the shepherd boy would rarely have had any time to himself before noon. It would have been then that he wrote his poetry, and then that he lifted his prayers. And it would have been then that he practiced with his sling. Under an overhead sun there are no distorting shadows; the target would be vivid and clear.

During my college years, the Bradley Braves were one of the top basketball teams in the nation. For one thing, they never lost at home. I recall going down to Peoria to play their freshman team during my first year at Wheaton. Even though our game was before the varsity battle, I soon came to understand why they were so tough at home. Their fans were delirious; the noise was mind-boggling, and the stands were filled with red towels ceremoniously waved when the Braves did something right and, more appropriately in our case, when the opponents did something wrong. We lost by thirty points.

There is a close relationship between the home-court advantage and peak-performance planning. Whereas we cannot control what others do, we can usually determine when and even where we will respond. That's a sound action activity and a key behavioral adjustment in the face of a crisis.

THE GRACE OF PACE

You know, there is a great parallel between the experience of choosing hope in the midst of a crisis and deep-sea diving. Both involve a sudden change in environment marked by an inordinant increase in pressure. Even so, we can learn something from the pattern of the divers. Having been subjected to enormous pressure, they must be very careful about resurfacing, to avoid "the bends." They ascend from the deep slowly and intentionally, with plenty of stops along the way.

Emerging from crisis calls for similar behavior. Things will not "snap" back into place, and they will *never* be exactly the same. Dr. Karl Slaikeu (whose book *The Phoenix Factor* has been a major resource for me) says: "You should expect disorganization, emotional flare-ups, unusual behavior, and feelings of helplessness and confusion. These are normal reactions to the severe trauma of a crisis. The trick is learning how to manage the feelings and control the erratic behavior, until life evens out once more" (*The Phoenix Factor*, p. 10).

So the challenge is to keep moving, but to do it at your own pace. And remember, that choice is your choice.

I think of the college student who contracted an inoperable terminal cancer. He established an ongoing relationship with the Reverend John Powell at Loyola University. Together, they worked through his anger, frustration, and denial. At last, Father Powell led him to consider the ultimate response to all human calamity, love.

Apparently, the boy's father had chosen to deal with the crisis through a crisp, executive analysis and retreat. Whenever he spoke to his son it was about the doctor's advice, or the effect of the medication, or the conditions at the treatment center. Having determined with Father Powell that it would be very sad to go through life and leave this world without ever telling those you love that you love them, the young man purposed to talk to his father.

He approached him in the family room one evening after supper. Dad was locked behind the evening paper, standard-operating-procedure.

"Dad."

"Yes, what?" he said without lowering the paper.

"Dad, I would like to talk with you."

"Well, talk."

"I mean . . . It's really important."

And the newspaper fluttered to the floor revealing something the boy had never seen before, his father's face covered with tears. They hugged each other and talked until dawn even though Dad had to be off to work at eight-fifteen in the morning.

Conquering crisis calls for that kind of confrontation. Some sage once observed, "Logic won't change an emotion—action will."

Often, during the course of my ministry, I have confessed to my affection for and identification with Peter, the impetuous disciple. In concluding this book I want to identify with him again and invite you to do the same. The scene is the Upper Room. The Master has just finished washing the disciples' feet, and he tells his friends that he must leave. Instantly Peter protests, "Oh no, you don't, I'm going with you!" Smiling, the Lord touches his hand and utters these words—they belong to every person who has ever chosen hope in the midst of crisis, to all of us ordering double-cheese and sausage pizzas:

Let not your hearts be troubled; believe in God, believe also in me. In my Father's house are many rooms; if it were not so, would I have told you that I go to prepare a place for you? And when I go and prepare a place for you, I will come again and will take you to myself, that where I am you may be also. And you know the way where I am going. . . .

I will not leave you desolate; I will come to you. Yet a little while, and the world will see me no more, but you will see me; because I live, you will live also. (John 14:1-4, 18-19)

HOPE ON COURSE

So it is time to put a bow on these thoughts, to place them in the sun of your mind where they might find nourishment and take root in your soul. When I first considered writing about hope I had no idea how broadly my brush would stroke. Now, looking back at all the subjects I have touched, concepts I have investigated, and issues I have raised, I am convinced, once again, that the Holy Spirit charted my course. When we believe in the power of God to overcome death it changes our perspective on everything. Even the suggestion that the wanderings of humanity might be cleansed and coordinated by the hand of one who lives forever, loving unconditionally, bolsters the faith with which we address the issues of our time. In these pages I have sought to underscore the relative significance of human experience, the critical role of attitude in issues of faith, the wisdom of creative risk, the promise of "the fullness of time," and the inclusive nature of the love of Christ. Through these lenses we have examined tragedy, oppression, innovation, and crisis. In the midst of it all, I have tried to be true to the admonition of the old gospel hymn, which says,

Turn your eyes upon Jesus,
Look full in His wonderful face,
And the things of earth will grow strangely dim
In the light of His glory and grace.
(Helen Lemel, "Turn Your Eyes Upon Jesus")

Would that more of us had the courage to reach for tomorrow. Would that more of us so understood the power and love of Jesus Christ as to trust in his presence as a launching pad from which no horizon is beyond reach. Would that humanity might so anchor in hope that peace and joy and the life abundant were more than rusted ideals.

Not long ago I was sharing a cup of coffee with a man who I believe will one day be recognized as one of the world's noted architects. Already he has designed award-winning buildings all over the globe. He is brilliant. As architects go, he is young. And he is driven. As we talked, I asked him about his life's goal. He stared into the distance before answering in a barely distinquishable whisper, "I want to make a seminal contribution to architecture." Stunned at the magnitude of such an intent, I said nothing for several minutes.

The world needs seminal contributions. Whence cometh hope? I am driven to instill it in the soul of humanity. I could write much more. Others have written before me, and I am sure there will be more to come. Still, hope, like so many issues of the heart, must be claimed in order to be empowered. The moment comes when one must set aside the travel guides and take the trip. Through these pages it has been my purpose to share the pictures, recall the legends, and chart the terrain of this land called hope. Having lived there for a long time, it was easy for me. I believe hope is most accessible through a personal friendship with Jesus Christ. To that end, it is my earnest prayer you will book passage with him to the land of hope, soon. I have found him to be the most caring and forgiving of all life's tour guides. Come to know him and, through him, choose hope.